MANAGING CHANGE IN LIBRARIES AND INFORMATION SERVICES:

a systems approach

MANAGING CHANGE IN LIBRARIES AND INFORMATION SERVICES:

a systems approach

PETER G. UNDERWOOD

CLIVE BINGLEY   LONDON

© Peter G. Underwood

Published by
Library Association Publishing Ltd
7 Ridgmount Street
London WC1E 7AE

First published 1990

British Library Cataloguing in Publication Data

Underwood, Peter G.
    Managing change in libraries and information services : a
    systems approach.
    1. Libraries. Management
    I. Title
    025.1

    ISBN 0-85157-451-3

Typeset in 10/12pt Times by Library Association Publishing Limited
Printed and made in Great Britain by Bookcraft (Bath) Ltd

To
Alice
at the beginning
and to
Zoë
at the end
but to my
parents
always

Contents

Preface

Discussion with many library and information service managers at home and overseas reveals that most are concerned, even worried, about change. This attitude is not confined to our profession: it is a concern shared by most managers. Strategic approaches to the management of change need to be developed if the services we provide are to remain responsive to the needs of users; managers must feel confident about the projects they supervise if they are to retain a sense of job satisfaction. Change needs to be viewed as a challenge but also as a normal part of managerial life rather than as a problem or a disease requiring treatment for its suppression.

The problems of managing change emerge in all organizations, regardless of the type of technology in use. This book is not confined to discussing 'computery' problems; it takes the special characteristics of the information world as its context but the techniques discussed could also be applied elsewhere. It is sometimes said that in developing a solution some 10% of the difficulties are technical: this book is mostly concerned with the remaining 90%.

The stimulus for the writing of this book was the development of the Systems Studies module of the Distance Learning Masters Degree Programme at the College of Librarianship, Wales. This development was exciting and encouraged me to collate a lot of information gathered during teaching and consultancy work. The confines of the course units limited what could be used and so the idea of a book took shape.

Thanks are due to Malcolm Tunley who commented on the early chapters and Don Mason who recognized the need for the Distance Learning Programme. Also to the many who have contributed unwittingly to what follows through their conversation and discussion during tutorials and meetings. If an occasional incident or problem is recognized, no direct criticism of the reader is intended: rather, it is a recognition that every manager faces similar issues. Perhaps Douglas Adams, the author of *The hitchhiker's guide to the galaxy* (London, Pan, 1979), is correct and we are *all* part of the ultimate case study.

Peter G. Underwood
Talybont, July 1990

Acknowledgements

Permission from copyright holders to reproduce the following illustrations is gratefully acknowledged:

Figures 4 to 6, from D. I. Cleland and W. R. King's *Systems analysis and project management*, 3rd ed., published by the McGraw-Hill Book Company.
Figures 13 to 16 and 18, from the *Data processing documentation standards*, published by the National Computing Centre.

1 *The systems approach to management*

The managerial culture

What is meant by the use of the word 'system'? To start with a definition might appear to be an easy and logical approach to the subject of this book but, as so often in life, the easy path can quickly lead into a quagmire. The problem lies in trying to define something which is not tangible: one cannot touch or point to it. The word 'system' represents a concept, not an entity.

Setting aside, for the moment, this question of definition, consider instead some of the concerns which attract the attention of managers of libraries and information services today. The development of information technology offers new means of serving users but which facilities will best suit their needs? How much will need to be spent to provide a sensible range of facilities? How can this expenditure be justified? Can the effectiveness of these new facilities be demonstrated? In a time of increasing concern about the quality of life, are staff satisfied with their jobs? Do highly trained, professional staff find adequate scope for exercising their talents? Does the organization help or hinder staff to manage the resources at their disposal? Are users satisfied with the delivery and range of services? Do those who hold the purse-strings perceive the services provided as being important and are they confident that the services represent a good investment of money? These and many other concerns present the profession with an increasingly complex task: how best to allocate resources and organize the provision of library and information services.

Management of any organization has become more complex because the world outside the organization intrudes much more than used to be the case. Legislation controls many aspects of employment, conditions of service and the working environment. Users are often encouraged by pressure groups within society to demand better, or different, services.

1

Those responsible for allocating funds have to justify expenditure to taxpayers or investors. Staff are aware of job opportunities elsewhere and are able to compare working conditions and rewards.

Libraries and information services are no exception to these intrusions. The pressure to justify expenditure on them has been a constant feature of managerial life. The early history of the public library movement contains many accounts of disputes about the necessity of providing services and much time was spent in statistical comparison between rival library authorities. The debate has continued, though sometimes at a muted level, to the present day. Similar instances of disputes about the value of services can be found in the academic library, special library and information service sectors.

The pressure to justify may not be new but its origin and manifestation are changing. Information technology is multiplying the channels through which information can flow from the originator to the user and some channels can circumvent libraries and information services as traditionally conceived. The provision of information on databases is a good example: a glance at popular computer and business journals will reveal many articles explaining how to use networks to establish contact with the host services providing the databases and how to select and search an appropriate database. Those providing the services are aware of the growing number of 'end-user' searchers and are gradually adapting the query languages and retrieval methods to make them more readily comprehensible. Libraries and information services are no longer a necessary feature of life for all information users, if they ever were.

Society has changing expectations, too. The multiplication of media has obviously increased the ways in which people can satisfy an information need or simply enjoy themselves. Most libraries and information services have responded by stocking audiovisual and other media; some have promoted their use in advance of great public awareness or interest. The power and uses of information are also more in the public eye: the rise of the 'consumer society' has fostered an increase in the demand for information related to the rights of individuals. Libraries and other information services, such as the Citizen's Advice Bureaux, have also responded to this need.

Professionally, the nature of work in library and information services has changed and is continuing to change. There can be few information workers who will not, at some time in their professional lives, make use of computers or of the products that the computer revolution has spawned. For many, the use of computers is an everyday occurrence:

wordprocessing, gaining access to information on databases, electronic mail, and the use of facsimile transmission are a few examples of the uses to which this technology has been put. It is interesting to note that many of these uses do not constitute novel approaches to the provision of services, though technology may enhance or increase the speed of them. Electronic mail is a new way of sending messages using technology but its use still results in a message arriving in a mailbox, albeit electronic. The essential nature of the service, passing information from one location to another, is not changed: the new technology frequently complements, rather than replaces, the existing.

The temptation for the manager introducing a new technology may be to assume that the previous pattern of services can, and should, continue without change apart from a welcome increase in speed, reduction in costs or other tangible benefits. There are dangers in giving in to this temptation. First, to assume that past practices represent satisfactory service and good value is quite unwarranted without some investigation. Secondly, the use of new technology may afford opportunities to offer something new. The development of online information retrieval, for example, could have been seen as the need to automate searching under authors, titles and subjects in an electronic form of catalogue or index. Instead, an opportunity was recognized: the use of computers could enhance the range of retrieval keys far beyond that usually considered feasible or economic in card catalogues and printed indexes, to include such novelties as word proximity searching and searching on publication dates.

A third danger in using the past as a model for the future is the perception of the service by the user. When computers were an uncommon and suitably impressive sight, their use by an organization was often publicized. Some firms built computer suites on the ground floor of their offices and put the machines and their operators on public view. Advertisements might include some reference to computer use. It is apparent that prospective customers were being invited to enter the modern world by association with the organization and its products. The expectations of such customers were raised and they might assume that the improvements of which the organization boasted should extend to all the services provided. In the mind of the customer the nature of the service, that is the package of benefits, goods, and feelings associated with using the organization, had changed. The technology in use and on public display enhanced the image of the service. This change in perception could be quite a handicap if the organization was, in fact, only using a computer system to process the payroll – an activity unlikely to affect anyone other than the employees. To the customer, the conjunction of bright, sparkling, new technology and a level of service little better than in the past could lead swiftly to disillusionment and discontent. To the staff having to deal with customers, the raised expectations could lead to frustration and lowered morale because of their inability to provide an enhanced level of service.

Although the computer is now a commonplace item in libraries and information centres the problem of user expectations often remains unsolved and, sometimes, unrecognized. Despite many anecdotes about the failures of modern technology, users tend to assume that a service will be improved with its use. Staff may also share such expectations before having full working experience.

The changes to library and information services consequent upon the development and use of new technology are complex and involve alterations to working practices, working relationships, attitudes and levels of expertise as well as technical changes to processes and equipment. Thus, it is best to view them as manifestations of 'socio-technic' change since this should remind the manager that technological changes, however small, will also have an effect on the social aspects of the working environment. Both aspects, the technological and the social, are the subject of change.

The discussion so far has centred on the use of new technology but the points made could apply, equally well, to any change in an organization: a change of personnel, change of method, change of building, even a change of name. There is an increased pressure on the manager to justify and account for what is done.

The manager is thus confronted with a difficulty: there may be pressure from without and within the organization to change to meet the challenge offered by competitors and to achieve new targets for the beneficial use of resources. Change can lead to enhanced services and improved efficiency but it also brings problems. Such problems are rarely confined to one aspect of a service but are likely to affect staff, users, competitors, suppliers, organizational arrangements and structures and so on. Yet, change can hardly be avoided if an organization is to remain vital and healthy. The greatest task for modern management of all kinds of enterprise is the productive management of change.

The systems approach to management provides a framework and body of techniques for accomplishing change which also recognizes its inherent difficulty and the problems which change may create. Change can also

4

offer opportunities and the systems approach provides a means of encouraging managers to identify, investigate, evaluate and promote such opportunities. Use of the systems approach should inculcate an active style of management: one which seeks to develop the organization and constantly explores avenues for this to be achieved.

Management of libraries and information centres in the modern world *is* more complex because they are more complex as organizations and because the environment in which they are found is itself more complex. More is demanded of them by society and there are many ways in which some of the information and cultural needs of society can be met. This complexity and the pressure to satisfy needs in an efficient manner has increased the challenge of library and information service management.

Meeting this challenge calls for certain key qualities. First, technical understanding: that is, a knowledge of how, in a particular enterprise, resources and processes are utilized to complete tasks. An astute manager recognizes that the right of access to resources will, ultimately, have to be justified: some attention must be given to the questions 'why do we need these resources?', 'do we still need them?' and 'could greater benefit be derived from using them in some other way?' Greater attention has been given by library and information service managers to these questions recently because assumptions about the worth of such services to society have been challenged. Being accountable also encourages a manager to pay attention to the way in which resources are used in the various processes of the enterprise. The efficiency with which resources are used and the effectiveness of the resultant service in meeting the needs of users have become important preoccupations. They have, of course, always been a concern of the manager but they did not necessarily occupy the primary place which society and organizational culture now dictates.

The second characteristic of the successful manager is an understanding of the basic ideas and principles of management. These form part of the core of professional studies for librarianship and information science. There is a danger, though, in assuming that pursuing such studies will produce managers. There is a limit to the amount of theory which can be included within the curriculum of a first-qualification course and sound arguments for limiting that exposure to what is likely to be useful during the early years of a professional career. In any case, absorbing a body of theoretical knowledge and practical techniques will not turn the student into a manager of a library or information service unless significant time is given for the new professional to develop confidence and experience. Training is a vital adjunct to professional education and an essential part

5

of the training is the inculcation of the belief that every professional is, in some sense, a manager of resources, shares a collective responsibility for the success of the service and is accountable for resource usage.

An interpersonal style which enables the manager to get things done *through* other people is the third characteristic. 'Getting ordinary people to do extraordinary things', a phrase coined many years ago, describes the art, as distinct from the science, of management. Part of that art is the skill of leadership. Leaders are not always good managers but they can convey a sense of enthusiasm and urgency to those who do possess the necessary management skills. However, for any manager the ability to lead, when necessary, is an essential skill, the successful exercise of which depends on having decided in what direction it is preferential for the organization to go. Interpersonal style then becomes an important quality if others are to share in the process of change. They must be convinced of the need for change and that the proposed direction of change is apposite and within the competence of the organization.

Fourthly, a manager must possess an ability to plan in the long and medium terms as well as being able to react to short term and urgent matters. One of the difficulties of managerial life is learning to set priorities; so many matters present themselves as being 'urgent' that it is easy to spend the majority of the available time on dealing with them. Such behaviour may, indeed, appear to be approved by senior people responsible for the funding of the organization: the service appears to be responsive and efficient because action follows on closely after 'urgent' matters have been raised. What is concealed by this responsiveness is that it is essentially a *reaction* to events which is devoid of much, if any, consideration of longer-term effects. Such a 'fire-fighting' approach to management will work for a short time: the blazes will be extinguished but the deep-rooted, smouldering, fire will continue to burn and erupt in unexpected places.

These qualities need to be present for the development of most organizations, but it is probably too much to expect that one person will have them all or that they will be equally important in every enterprise. For example, the pace of change experienced by a small library or information service attached to an organization concerned with research might be great: the need to match the collections and services to emerging research areas would predicate the need for a close involvement of information workers with the appropriate research teams. The managerial emphasis should be on planning to accommodate such changes as quickly as possible. There might be less need to emphasize leadership skills because of the small number of information workers involved. A converse example would be an academic library providing services to faculties teaching a traditional pattern of studies: the pace of change experienced by the library could be slower and there might not be the need to emphasize close involvement of library staff with teaching teams. The need to facilitate change would, however, still be an important role for the manager and would require a concentration on the task of leadership.

To explore these ideas further consider an aspect of psychology. A person's perception of the world is thought to be formed by beliefs, attitudes and the surrounding culture during the formative years of life. Changes in the environment and the acquisition of experience lead to modifications of perception, but this is a fairly slow process. Perception tends to predicate the type of response the person will offer to new circumstances which daily life presents. Some people, for example, respond more strongly to challenges about how to *do* things than others: such people tend to be 'task-oriented' and may be rather more interested in completing some work than in the reactions of people around them. Others have a strong response to people: for them, the task is almost a vehicle for watching and participating in the complexity of human behaviour. There is a strong similarity here in the contrast between the early twentieth-century preoccupation with 'scientific management', which emphasized careful design and measurement of work, and the more recent 'behavioural approach' to management which emphasizes the need to foster motivation of individuals through jobs designed to meet their needs for social satisfaction and a degree of autonomy. The contrast has been well explored by Jones[1].

The distinction between perceptions is not dichotomous: rather, there is a spectrum ranging from 'people orientation' to 'task orientation' and most people can be found somewhere between the two extremes. The idea has been elaborated by Blake and Mouton[2] in their Managerial Grid, which was developed as a training aid for managers. The Managerial Grid method depends on analysing the characteristics and behaviour to be expected from various management styles, comparing them and then seeking to define the behavioural requirements for shifting from one style to another. A particular focus is the distinction between concern for people and concern for task completion. The aim is to increase the range of styles a manager can employ rather than enforcing a permanent change from one to another. The Managerial Grid thus recognizes that the appropriate style depends upon the problem being faced. The greatest aid in this kind of personal management development is to know what one's own characteristics are and to what factors one tends to respond strongly or weakly. It is also of value to know this when trying to build a management team. In a service managed and run by one person much of the success will depend on the willingness and ability of that person to balance the various demands inherent in the job. Management style in such circumstances will inevitably result in a service with a distinctive character − one which some customers will favour and others will reject. With a team, however, because there are several personalities involved, there is the potential for creating a service which is bland but more broadly acceptable. That potential is realized by consciously trying to build a team with complementary strengths.

Enterprises are manifestly different as to their technical content, their economies and organization sizes, the degree of contact with customers, their environmental impact and so on. Studies suggest that differences in managerial style can be linked to differences in the culture of enterprises[3]. Research tends to show that, for example, in a successful manufacturing company the type of technology used, the degree of uncertainty and the unpredictable nature of the production task determine the kind and level of control needed. This level of control, in turn, affects the organizational structure, management style and behaviour. Additionally, there seems to be no best way to organize an enterprise. Thus, it may be concluded that successful management involves recognizing what style tends to be most suitable, most of the time, for the kind of enterprise being run, but there must also be a recognition that other styles may suit particular circumstances: their selection is, in other words, contingent upon the circumstances[4]. There is no reason to suppose that variant styles are not also important in libraries and information services and considerable variations in style are, in practice, to be found.

The service enterprise
Much library and information work forms part of what might be called a 'service enterprise': that is to say, there are not many librarians or information workers who rely directly on the sale of information or information-related products to earn a living. Instead there is a reliance on using resources, including skills and talents, to enhance or facilitate the use by others of information. The word 'information' here includes anything that might be thought of as a legitimate source: novels, reference books, databases, catalogues, computer software, audiovisual material and so on. Librarians and information workers are intermediaries and

their services are of value because users recognize that life can be made easier or more pleasant through the use of these services. The problems that arise when attempts are made to measure the effectiveness of such services are beyond the scope of this introductory chapter, but it should be noted that attempts at such measurements present considerable difficulties principally because these services do not produce a very concrete end-product. They produce, instead, states or sensations: the state of being better informed, the sensation of being entertained by reading a book or viewing a video-cassette. Unless some means of assigning a value to these can be decided, there is no way of answering questions about the quantitative effectiveness of services and scarcely any possibility of saying much about their quality.

Library and information work rarely constitutes the whole, or even the major part, of the work of an organization. Certainly it is possible to think of a university library as functioning as an autonomous unit. One could perceive it as receiving an input of money and a set of goals from the environment of, say, the university authorities, but how it sets about achieving those goals and spending the money might seem to be largely under its own control. This is something of an illusion: the degree of autonomy is severely constrained by external factors, such as the policy of the university, auditing and legal requirements, professional and social acceptability, and internal factors, such as levels of staffing and the (sometimes erroneous) expectation by users and staff that existing services will be largely maintained as before. A similar argument prevails for the commercial or 'special' library, though the more precise definition of the target user group, (researchers, executives and so on) means that the external factors may exercise an even greater influence because the range of needs may be considered to be fairly tightly determined. The *operating* environment, then, as well as the internal environment, is of major importance for a service enterprise.

So far, it has been suggested that, as a manager, the librarian or information worker will have to cope with a considerable degree of complexity in running a library and information service. Information − or the kind of feeling that can be engendered by using information − is an intangible product; it is supplied to a user who may be aware or unaware of need; the service is usually maintained against a background of some external financial and other control. Now add to this the technological changes occurring as we move from a print-based technology to the use of electronic systems and information technology. The result is an environment which has become increasingly challenging to conventional library and information services because there are several pathways to apparent satisfaction. Consider, for example, the in-house company information service providing specialized information to employees of the firm. Over the years some expertise in online searching may have been developed and an internal company information database may also have been established as part of its work. The installation of a computer-based data communications network throughout the company premises makes this database accessible to company research staff from their own terminals, if they so wish. Perhaps they also become aware of external databases and begin to use them. The role of the information service as anything other than the provider of an internal database seems to be threatened by this development. How should the information services manager respond? Perhaps by protesting about a possible explosion of costs because of inefficient searching by end-users? But what proof is there that experts in searching provide a better and more cost-effective service? Perhaps, instead, the response should be to recognize the need for a different kind of information service: one which undertakes the training of end-users to improve their searching performance. Another possibility would be for the information service to become involved in the specification and design of an intelligent link to databases, to facilitate searching by relatively unskilled end-users, coupled with a cost-recording function. Such approaches build positively on a perceived challenge or threat, turning it into an opportunity.

The manager of a library or information service, then, is concerned with an objective consideration of the future which recognizes the importance of revealing the expectations and assumptions of the organization and integrating them with a careful analysis of the operating and internal environments. This analysis must extend to the 'people' aspects as well as to tasks. It must also attempt to reveal the means by which judgements of effectiveness and efficiency might be made.

The systems approach
The systems approach can provide a useful framework for the manager concerned with an objective consideration of the future. Erich Jantsch[5] has elaborated this idea by proposing a framework, or model, which defines the activity of planning along four dimensions, called 'horizontal', 'vertical', 'time and causality' and 'action'.

Impact on society in terms of:	Impact on:
Culture	Individuals
Psychology	Single events
Technology	
etc.	

Macro level	Micro level

Figure 1 Horizontal dimension of planning

The *horizontal* dimension (Figure 1) is concerned with the problem of system complexity. In analysing any management proposal it is possible to look at the likely effects at a macro level, where all the social, cultural, psychological, technical and other impacts that can be identified are taken into account. This is the complex view. It is often helpful to restrict one's view to a micro level, concentrating on just a few of the impacts – perhaps those that are believed to be principally involved in the proposed change. The systems approach reminds planners that, having analysed at the micro level, it is necessary to return to the macro level and check that what was considered workable at the micro level will also be workable at the macro level. This is greatly facilitated by first spending time in identifying those who have some interest in, or concern for, the service (the term 'stakeholders' is often used to describe them) and considering the relationship between the service and the environment in which it has to operate. The horizontal dimension also reveals that a variety of different views and opinions may be held about the characteristics of a system and that these may be irreconcilable. What is good at the macro level of society may have a damaging effect on the life and happiness of individuals; conversely, changes to make a small process more efficient may have a deleterious effect on the complete system. This dimension, then, can be understood as emphasizing the need for discussion and dialectic to establish what views are held.

The *vertical* dimension (Figure 2) emphasizes the need to consider planning at *policy*, *strategic* and *operational* levels. The *policy* level is concerned with the achievement of objectives of the system, expressed in broad behavioural terms rather than as quantitative goals; it has sometimes been called the 'ought to' level of planning. Such objectives cannot be attained once and forever but serve as enduring guides for other levels of planning. For example, a company information service might state that its policy is: 'to serve the needs of research staff and

11

Figure 2   Vertical dimension of planning

senior managers for information about the company's and its competitors' products and suitable markets and to furnish information associated with the development of new company products'. The objectives might also be ranked, perhaps in terms of how quickly they may be achieved, their perceived urgency, or their perceived importance to the system and the corporate environment.

The *strategic* level (the 'can do' level) is concerned with the achievement of specific goals. At this level, the objectives are taken as fixed, and the manager is concerned principally with translating them into outcomes, seeking the optimum strategy amongst several strategic options. In the previous example, information about markets might be gained from sources such as market reports and suitable statistical and demographic databases. Factors such as cost, time taken to supply information, convenience and confidentiality would form part of the assessment leading to the choice of strategy. Taking these two levels of *policy* and *strategy* together, there is a recognition that there may be several ways of achieving policy objectives but the role of the manager is to select the best strategic path according to some quantitative criterion.

At the *operational* level (the 'will' level), planning activity is concerned with attaining fixed strategic targets such as levels of growth or the development of new services. In particular, the focus is on the allocation and arrangement of resources, or inputs, to the system. This is the level at which 'ends and means', or tactics, are defined. The allocation is guided by the strategic plan, derived from the policy and strategy levels, but mediated by the need to use the resources committed to the project as efficiently as possible. Thus, to continue with the previous example, knowing that one searcher is more skilled than another in using particular databases would influence the manager in allocating project tasks to members of staff.

Successful planning requires that there be a continuous interaction between these three levels. Policy objectives lead to the development of strategic goals which determine operational targets but resource availability and disposition may necessitate adjustment of strategies. A large increase in price for using particular databases might, for example, encourage the manager in the example to select another route to the required information. Major price rises, coupled with uncertainty about staff availability, might persuade the manager to consult the parent company about a shift in policy for the information service, perhaps no longer seeking to supply information to all sectors of the company's research staff.

Planning is intrinsically concerned with the future. The *time* and *causality* dimension (Figure 3) is concerned with reconciling two modes of forecasting. The first mode is simple extrapolation from the present state, sometimes called 'normative' forecasting because it assumes that the past is a good predictor of the future and that prevailing conditions will continue to apply. There will be an evident link between existing operations and planned operations; normative forecasting seeks to exploit this link by reviewing factors which influenced past performance and assessing the likely effect of these factors on such plans.

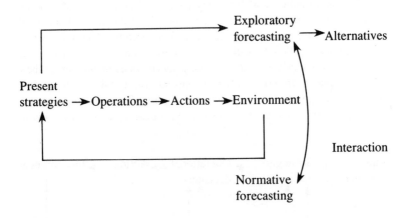

Figure 3   Time and causality dimension of planning

13

The second mode is concerned with exploratory forecasting, where a future beyond existing constraints is contemplated. It is characterized by the question: 'where are we now and where do we want to be?' Because the constraints are removed, if only in the imagination, the level of risk is greater. Less is known, more is unpredictable; the effect of conditions, previously thought significant, may be less clear. Depending on their attitudes to risk, managers may be more or less willing to indulge in exploratory forecasting. It is important to recognize that both views are necessary for an organization to grow and to continue to serve the needs of its stakeholders. The manager needs a 'rich picture' of both the predicted and the tenable futures to ensure that eventual plans are neither pedestrian nor unrealistic. New ideas and novel approaches are risky: an over-reliance on normative forecasting, which places emphasis on the past as a predictor of the future, may lead the manager to neglect opportunities for profitable and interesting development. Exploratory forecasting assumes great importance when developing a strategic approach to introducing new technology. One does not need to replicate past methods: something better may be achievable with the new technology. On the other hand, too much emphasis on exploratory forecasting may lead the manager to neglect the improvement of services based on well-known techniques.

The final dimension in Jantsch's model, that of 'action' (Figure 4), refers to the interaction between planning and implementation. Planning should lead to action and the consequences of action should provide feedback for further strategic and operational considerations. Traditional planning is often locked into dealing with symptoms. The approach is often, in jest, called 'fire-fighting' but the truth is that studies[6] of managerial work demonstrate that many managers habitually spend their time in coping with day-to-day problems and rarely take the long view of where their part of the organization is going. The systems approach to planning should lead the manager from dealing with symptoms to

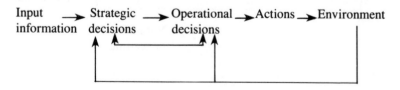

Figure 4 Action dimension of planning

14

dealing with underlying problems and then on to opportunities, thus developing a pro-active rather than a solely reactive attitude. The approach may seem quite complex, especially when considered in the abstract, but its use should inculcate a set of attitudes in the manager which, to extend the metaphor, extends interests from day-to-day fire-fighting to the productive use of fuel and even to solar energy!

The model is now complete. It is important to recognize that no single dimension, or incomplete combination of dimensions, can give a satisfactory view of the problem of planning which confronts the manager. Only when taken together, complete and entire, can the model begin to provide a suitable framework for thinking about planning. One should also be aware that a model is an abstraction of reality: it can only ever reflect certain characteristics, thought to be important by its builder. It is not a substitute for reality. Jantsch's model will not cope with describing everything the manager has to do but it should not be regarded, either, as an ornate stairway to an 'ivory tower'. The astute manager discovers when such models are useful and to what extent they may be relied upon. They are added to an armoury of techniques to complement other weapons rather than to supplant them.

It is also important to recognize that the model depends on a conscious effort to design managerial structures which can gather the information needed and pass it back (usually termed 'feedback') to components of the model. For example, the link in the action dimension (Figure 4) between actions and operational decisions implies some means of detecting the effect of actions on the environment and of communicating that effect to those responsible for making operational decisions. When setting up new projects, an important part of the planner's job will be to decide what effects it is desirable, and possible, to measure and to consider how, when and to whom such effects shall be made known.

Faced with this rather complicated task, some managers might remark that this is very well if one is faced with running a large service, with many departments, service points, many people and diverse responsibilities. A very serious-minded approach to planning, with detailed attention to control methods and structure, would be absolutely necessary. But what if one is running a much smaller-scale service? Surely these techniques are unnecessary? Consider this: however large or small the enterprise, it is a professional responsibility to ensure that resources are used to create *effective* services. Because the environment tends to change, the type of services needed may also change. Only through some disciplined approach to planning can one ensure that opportunities are recognized. The small-scale enterprise may not need a complicated planning structure, with committees, formal reporting guidelines and so on but the discipline it enforces *is* needed. It is simply too easy, otherwise, to neglect the tasks of evaluation and planning.

The productive use of information technology and other new techniques to service provision represents a major challenge for all libraries and information services. As the speed of technical development increases it is important for us, as managers, to assess what is likely to be useful and then to manage its introduction. It is also important for managers to recognize that the use of technology will change jobs and will demand of people the use of different skills. It will not necessarily make life better, in any objective sense, but it will make life different and it is part of that managerial responsibility to prepare people for change. Only an approach to development which takes into account the people, the technology and the environment − an approach which encourages a strategic view − is likely to succeed: it is to this end that the systems approach was developed.

What is a 'system'?

Having considered briefly what is meant by the term 'systems approach' it is appropriate to return to the problem of defining the word 'system'. The problem, as mentioned at the start of this chapter, arises from the intangibility of the concept and, thus, the difficulty of creating a suitable description. This should not dissuade us from using the word: everyday life is full of instances where words, such as 'love' or 'rich', are used without any attempt at precise definition. These and similar words are usually attached to examples of behaviour or states which the onlookers agree exhibit the necessary characteristics. No dictionary would attempt to define 'rich' by listing a set of possessions or an income level as criteria but, by agreement, a group could decide that some people were rich whilst others were not.

The word 'system' has become a common term, often applied to things which seem large or complex. It is *so* frequently encountered, that it can become quite difficult to decide what it means even within a defined context. When a manufacturer of washing powder, computer programmers, doctors, economists, astronomers and ecologists use the same word, 'system', in describing their interests, can anyone be sure what they mean? What is the connection between the solar system and the monetary system? Do the skeletal system and a computer system have anything in common? Can we sensibly compare the ecological system

16

of our planet and the 'brand-new washing system' of the detergent manufacturer? What does this word 'system' mean if it can be used in so many and different contexts? Perhaps the word is in danger of becoming trivialized: should these disparate things all attract the name of system? Is it possible for users of the word to agree on a meaning such that it can legitimately be used to describe both the vast and the minute, the natural and the fabricated, the technical and the social, the concrete and the abstract?

A comparison of various dictionary definitions of the word 'system' quickly reveals that compilers of dictionaries are no nearer agreement. In an interesting essay, Jordan[7] recounts that at a meeting of experts from various disciplines the participants found it very difficult to define the word, but, despite this impediment, their meeting was quite successful. He raises the point: how can we speak intelligently and interestingly about something which we cannot define?

The problem of definition is far from trivial, because if there is no agreement on how to use the word, then sensible discussion is likely to be impeded: if Humpty-Dumpty has his way and a word can mean what the user wishes it to mean, conversation will collapse in semantic confusion.

Jordan argues that there is a 'core meaning' to the word 'system': the word can be used to describe things which are seen, or thought of, as consisting of a set of parts connected in some distinguishable way. Whenever one person can indicate or describe a set of elements and how they are connected and can communicate this concept to another person, the use of the word 'system' would be an appropriate name for the thing under discussion.

Jordan considers that much of the confusion arises because the word 'system' is often used in a specific context whereas its proper context is in describing abstract or general qualities. He concludes that the only things which need be common to all uses of the word are that each system, so described, should have a collection of identifiable entities and identifiable connections between them. The many uses outlined above can be considered to be correct but not necessarily useful unless the elements forming each 'system' are also identified and there is some purpose in viewing them as a collective unit. There is little point in using the word solely for effect or in a bid to add a scientific gloss to the ordinary.

We can agree, then, that the word 'system' is difficult to define, but that it is possible to accept a general definition such as:

17

a set of parts and functions, sometimes called 'components', which are connected by a network of relationships or actions.

The pragmatist will probably wish to add that the set should have some defined purpose. Some writers underline this point by insisting that a system can be considered to be a collection of people, objects and activities about which it is meaningful to talk as if it has some unity. Churchman[8] also emphasizes this by suggesting that, to be described as a 'system', the thing under consideration must have objectives or purposes. Unfortunately, these may be quite difficult to discern: what, for example, are the objectives of the solar system? The nervous system undoubtedly has a purpose but how easy is it to express? Wyllys notes that the difficulty has prompted the comment that 'system is a group of things that operates at a level of complexity higher than the highest level that we think we understand'.[9] Within this seemingly facetious remark there is a core of truth because some discussions of systems verge on the metaphysical and have little practical value.

The definition outlined above will encompass both formal and informal structures; clearly library and information services, like most organizations, have both structures in evidence. The organization chart, so often believed to represent the organization, displays only one aspect: usually, the formal reporting and responsibility structure. The informal structure represents centres of power and influence, often based on people or groups with some sort of common interest. It is rare to find formal acknowledgement of the presence of an informal structure, although all are aware of it and use it. By acknowledging that the definition of 'system' can encompass both formal and informal structures the manager is reminded that changes will affect both and a strategy must be planned accordingly. The recognition may prompt the manager also to consider whether other structures, such as a set of user groups, are present.

The concept of 'system' thus drives us to a multi-dimensional view of an organization, with many structures existing simultaneously. It is rarely possible to deal with them together, because of the complexity of the managerial problems, and the systems approach encourages us to concentrate on the structure or structures considered salient at a particular time, but not to forget the 'big picture'.

The lack of a specific definition has another effect. It is vital to establish how the word is to be used within a particular context: for example, the library or information service manager's view of what set of people, objects and activities constitute the library system of a company may well be different from that of, say, the director of finance. Used properly, and with agreement, the word is useful and can serve to remind managers that organizations are complex and represent a subtle balance of objectives, tasks, personalities and events. Failure to define and agree on the constitution of the set of things comprising the particular system under discussion will lead only to confusion or, worse, resentment and defensiveness.

System components

In seeking to define a system in such a way that the definition can be used in discussion it is best to begin with trying to identify the system components; that is, the people, activities and events, and objects which together form that system. In essence the process of definition sets the components apart from their surroundings and encloses them within a boundary. This process of grouping is quite familiar. It forms part of the repertoire of responses which humans use for dealing with the complexity of life: 'home' is recognized as comprising a different set of entities from 'work' or 'social life'. This can sometimes be demonstrated quite dramatically: it may be difficult to name or even recognize a person if we see them in a context with which we do not usually associate them. Our perception has consigned them to one system and is reluctant to identify them within the boundary of another.

System boundaries are also subject to negotiation. Agreement on their nature and position is needed before further discussion can take place. The basis of the agreement will usually be a shared view of a distinction between internal and external goals of the organization or part of the organization under discussion. An internal goal can be considered to reflect ideas about the strategy and tactics of the organization, these being expressed in terms of how resources are controlled, whereas external goals reflect ideas about the effects of the work of the organization upon the environment. The external goals are concerned with things outside the system boundary. For an information service, for example, the user may be seen as outside the boundary because the availability of the service should *affect* the work methods of the user, but it is clear that those work methods are not under the *control* of the information service. The distinction between control and influence is a useful means of defining a system boundary. It is also capable of being used to separate parts of an organization: the cataloguing department of a university library and the reader services department can influence each other, perhaps by suggesting improvements in the provision of access points to the catalogue, but it is unlikely that one will be in a formal position to control the other and enforce its view. The process of definition of system boundaries may be seen as a process of identifying and describing 'spheres of influence'.

An additional aspect of the process of boundary identification is that it should aid the manager in preparing an organization for change. Components within the system boundary can be analysed, described and costed; their function can be fairly precisely defined and understood; their performance can be evaluated according to agreed standards. New targets can be set, new working methods can be tried and their effects assessed. Change in one part of the system can be monitored to detect its effects on other parts of the system. The manager is able to view the system as a whole and communicate with it. This may not be easy, or possible, for components outside the boundary. For example, consider an information service manager seeking to change the production methods for a current awareness bulletin. The work of the present production team may be well understood and carefully costed. Senior management of the parent organization responsible for the service may suggest the need for economies. The problem of high cost of production and changes likely to mitigate its effects may be discussed by the team, assessed and tested. A climate in which change is acceptable or can, at least, be discussed has been created. To the senior managers outside the information service system boundary the precise nature of the changes is unlikely to be important and may be incomprehensible without some knowledge of the present working methods: the principal concern of the senior managers is with the new costings for the information service and discussion with the information service manager will be in terms of those costings.

The senior managers may also be users of the current awareness bulletin. As such, their use of the bulletin may be affected adversely or beneficially by the changes. It is important for the information service manager to recognize that the role of user is here distinct from that of provider of resources. Bulletins are usually sent to many groups of staff within an organization and the consideration of their value and use must include all groups. Just because one user group appears to be very powerful should not predispose the information service manager to consider only the views of that group. This example highlights another important idea implicit in the systems approach: the identification of roles played by individuals and groups within and outside the system boundary. In many cases, multiple roles will be discernible, often played by the same people. In facilitating change, the manager has to understand that a proposed change is likely to affect each role differently: each individual or group playing a particular role will have different responses and will need to be treated distinctly by the manager. Even so, where multiple roles are played, the cumulative effects of change on the differing roles may produce some complicated and highly individual responses. It is well said that all change is a process of collective negotiation.

The notion of system components can be explored further with the aid of a systems model (Figure 5). This represents a simple systems model, one which shows the main flow of work and information about work around an organization. It is an abstract view: no detail about any component is given but the components and their links are emphasized and the nature of the system is summarized.

This view regards the organization as being an open system: the organization is linked to its environment by the passage of inputs, outputs and control signals. This is a critical point: General System Theory, as developed by Ludwig von Bertalanffy, makes a distinction between closed and open systems. The closed system has no links to the environment and will become moribund because it lacks the capacity to respond to changes in the environment. This may take a long time if the environment changes very slowly, but the lack of adaptation means that eventually the environment will become hostile to the closed system. The open system *is* linked to the environment and is stimulated to respond to changes in such a way that the system tends to survive. General System Theory has attempted to develop a series of theorems which link the behaviour of all systems − biological, organizational, mechanical and so on. For our purposes, the important point is that open systems must establish a means of monitoring the environment and assessing needs.

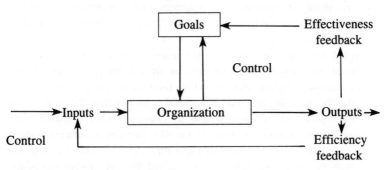

Figure 5 Simple systems model

21

In relation to libraries and information services, the community study and user study represent a major means of achieving this. It must be remembered, however, that these are formal, rather highly structured means of gathering information and that less formal channels are also useful. All information about how the library or information service and its efforts are perceived by users represents valuable information and emphasizes the link across the system boundary to the environment. It is almost impossible to think of a library or information service which would not be open to its environment in this way but the simple reception of information is not enough: for a system to be open, it must also respond to that information. Change, as we have seen, can be profoundly threatening but the tendency to explain away responses from users and not to change is a sure sign of closure in a system.

The simple systems model also illustrates the important feature of feedback of both effectiveness and efficiency. It is now a familiar notion to most managers that a regular review of efficiency (the degree to which resources are being used economically) and effectiveness (the degree to which the needs of the environment are being met) are a necessary part of any manager's job. There is a growing need to be able to demonstrate efficiency and effectiveness to those who provide the resources. The type of feedback specified by the simple systems model is 'negative feedback'. By sampling the output from the organization and comparing it with some criteria a decision can be made about whether to adjust the input in such a way as to make the output more satisfactory. The theory is that negative feedback leads to stability in a system because the system becomes self-correcting. This may be true of mechanical or biological systems, but one suspects that social systems may not respond quite so neatly: for example, how long might it take an information service to adjust its cataloguing practices, even supposing the manager could persuade the staff that users did not find them suitable? Nonetheless, the principle of frequent assessment of effectiveness and efficiency, coupled with the conviction that the results should be used rather than ignored, is a major point to be drawn from General System Theory.

For sensible management thinking, the simple systems model needs to be elaborated. In particular, it is useful to try to define the environment of the system more closely and to consider what constitutes the organization. One way of doing this is illustrated by a complex systems model (Figure 6). The model displays three environmental levels. The internal environment, which is contained by the system boundary, constitutes all of those elements or entities that are within the official

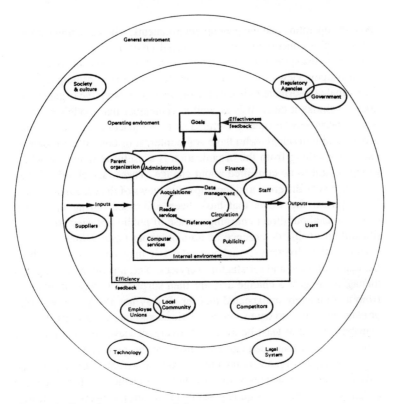

Figure 6 Complex systems model

jurisdiction of the organization. The internal environment is composed of subsystems, which operate within the context of the organization and which interact with each other. A change to one part of the system may affect the working of another, because of this linkage. Part of the work of analysing a system is concerned with the investigation of these linkages so that the effects of change can be more easily predicted.

The operating environment constitutes the group of suppliers, customers and interest groups which deal with, influence or are influenced directly by the work of the organization. The general environment constitutes the social, economic and technological context within which any organization operates. The organization has the greatest degree of control over its own internal environment, but the general environment is capable of exerting a strong influence through the operating environment. Strategic management requires information principally

23

about the operating and the general environments, whereas administration is principally concerned with the internal environment.

The complex systems model we have looked at presents only one aspect of the systems view of an organization. It is concerned principally with the formal task-oriented view of the organization: what the organization does, or thinks it does. It is as well to remember that models showing other aspects may be equally useful: a systems model showing the various groups and individuals who have some interest or commitment or who expect something from the organization is a useful reminder of which groups ought to be consulted about change. These 'stakeholders' may well have very different and incompatible views of the organization and its purposes: the views that have been expressed during the recent discussions about direct charging for use of public libraries are a good illustration of this divergence of opinion about basic values.

Unless this diversity is acknowledged it may be very difficult to maintain balanced and satisfactory services. Yet, it is often the case that managers suggest a change and are then surprised to have it attacked from a completely unexpected quarter. It may not always be possible, or even desirable, to try to satisfy all views and interest groups, but the manager should at least be aware of divergent views and the range of stakeholders so that adequate responses can be prepared.

In viewing the organization within the system we noted that the internal environment was made up of various entities or elements. These are often called 'subsystems'. It is quite possible to take each subsystem, consider it as a separate *system* and reveal subsystems within it. Figure 7 demonstrates this approach. It is almost like viewing an organism through

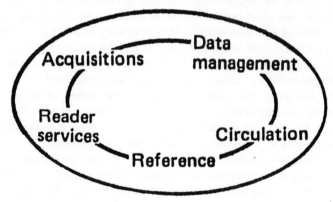

Figure 7   Subsystems model

24

a microscope at higher and higher levels of magnification. This approach enables one to recognize why the definition of system has to be so elastic: the system can be considered to be the complete organization (a university, for example), part of the organization (the university library), a separate process (acquisitions) or even one part of a process (standing orders). The definition of the boundary depends, in each case, on what it is sensible for the manager to study in relation to a particular problem. The systems approach reminds us of the need to consider a system in its environment and helps us to reveal the linkages to that environment and to other subsystems, but it does not enforce a particular standpoint.

Systems investigation stages
The task of investigation is implicit within systems thinking: it should, of course, be implicit in all management thinking, but there are many examples of decisions and, indeed, complete management strategies, which owe more to whim and 'flying by the seat of one's pants' than to any concerted effort at defining and analysing problems. Not that this is always wrong: there are plenty of occasions where the opportunity for careful analysis and considered decision-making is denied to the manager. It is not to be relied upon, however, as the major management style of an organization, especially where many people are involved, the environment presents social, financial or technological challenges or the future of the organization is rather uncertain.

Most investigations follow a rough pattern of phases of activity. The classical approach uses a framework often called the system or project life cycle. It is commonly described as having five consecutive stages, listed below:

(a) Feasibility study − problem recognition, technical survey and economic justification
(b) Analysis − determination of detailed requirements
(c) Design − development of design based on the analysis
(d) Implementation − construction, installation and full testing in workplace; staff training
(e) Operation − normal working; review of performance

Although most authors adhere to a core model covering these stages, many elaborate, split stages and re-name them. Miles[10] presents a full analysis of the terminological differences. The sequence outlined above is, however, adequate for general use.

The first stage of the sequence is concerned with recognizing that there

25

is a problem to be solved or that an opportunity for some project has presented itself which affects a system or part of a system within the internal environment of the organization. To decide whether it is worthwhile for the organization to respond to the challenge, a technical survey and economic justification has to be prepared. This first stage is known as a feasibility study. At the end of this stage, the manager should have sufficient information to decide whether it is worth committing further resources.

The second stage is that of analysis. Here, the detailed requirements of the project are discovered. This will often involve detailed analysis of existing procedures so that a complete understanding of the procedure and the way it is linked to other procedures within and outside the system is achieved.

The design of the new process occupies the next stage. Here, the analysis is used to guide the design, in particular where the new process will link with other, unchanged, processes. The object is to ensure that any necessary data, records or other information are still created and passed from the new to the existing systems.

The fourth stage is that of implementation, where the new design is used to construct the system which is then installed, tested in its workplace, the staff are trained and, if all is satisfactory, the system is handed over for the final phase, operation. This final phase should also include some review of system performance. The 'cycle' implies that the review may lead to another evolution.

In this form, the system life cycle bears a strong resemblance to the planning cycle, so often described in management textbooks: this is no accident, because planning and systems thinking are intrinsically connected with the idea of orderly, balanced management style. It is worth noting, though, that alternative methods, often called 'soft' techniques, have been developed. More will be said about these in succeeding chapters, where they will be contrasted with the classical approaches.

The management theorist Ackoff[11] once described the milieu of the manager as a 'mess' and the manager's job that of working in it, with its constituents. Perhaps most of us do work in a mess of social, personnel and technological problems which call for a wide variety of management styles and responses, but a little investigation of the mess would do much to aid our thinking before we plunge in, yet again.

Notes

1 Jones, K., *Conflict and change in library organizations: people, power and service*. London, Bingley, 1984, part 3, chapter 1.

2 Blake, R. R. and Mouton, J. S., *The managerial grid III*, 3rd ed., Gulf, 1984.

3 For a discussion of the impact of environment on organizations see Katz, D. and Kahn, R. L., *The social psychology of organizations*, 2nd ed., New York, Wiley, 1978, Chapter 5.

4 Katz, D. and Kahn, R. L., *The social psychology of organizations*, 2nd ed., New York, Wiley, 1978, 565-9.

5 Jantsch, E., 'Forecasting and systems approach: a frame of reference', *Management science*, **19**, (12), 1973, 1355-67.

6 Jones, K., *Conflict and change in library organizations: people, power and service*, London, Bingley, 1984, 117-21.

7 Jordan, N., 'Some thinking about "system"', *Systems thinking*, vol. 2, ed. F. E. Emery, Harmondsworth, Penguin Books, 1981, 15-39.

8 Churchman, C. W., *The systems approach*, New York, Dell, 1968, 29-30.

9 Wyllys, R. E., 'System design – principles and techniques', in *Annual review of information science and technology*, **14**, 1979, 4.

10 Miles, R. K., 'Computer systems analysis: the constraint of the hard systems paradigm', *Journal of applied systems analysis*, **12**, 1985, 55-65.

11 Ackoff, R. L., 'The art and science of mess management', *Interfaces*, **11**, 1981, 20-6.

2 *The role of management*

Power and leadership

It must often seem that the position of senior management is unenviable. There is a pressure to achieve ever higher standards of performance at lower cost and a strong trend in society towards including a wider spectrum of workers in management through consultation and participation in decision-making. Formulating policy and determining strategy are no longer solely the provinces of senior management yet it remains accountable for performance. The task of a leader can rarely be confused with that of an autocrat: instead, the leader is a facilitator, 'animateur' and coordinator of opinion and ideas. Changes can no longer be imposed.

The distinction is especially apparent if one compares management theory as derived from the work of Weber[1] with the work of the 'human relations school' of Mayo[2] and, later, Likert.[3] Weber, working at the beginning of the twentieth century, developed a model of bureaucracy (sometimes called 'machine' theory) which emphasized division of tasks for greater efficiency, standardization of the methods of performing tasks and a centralized, unified, role of making decisions inherent in a principle of legitimated authority. Control is exercised through a chain of command which is hierarchical and compliance is sought through a system of rewards for technical proficiency. The individual characteristics and personalities of those working within the bureaucracy are largely suppressed. Mayo, working in the 1920s, focused attention on the characteristics of the small, often informal, groups which employees quickly formed in the workplace. The operation of strict standards of behaviour (called 'norms') exercised a powerful means of control over group members which was independent of legitimate authority. Likert, writing in the 1960s, developed this idea and integrated it with the concept of formal organizational structures to create the notion of 'organizational families' where work groups are formed, often with overlapping membership, with formal leaders in each group acting as a link with the next higher level in the hierarchy. The group, acting with the leader, take decisions concerning the tasks to which they have been assigned. The progression apparent in these theories is from a unitary concept of leadership towards a pluralistic concept based more on negotiation than coercion.

The trend is especially marked in organizations, such as libraries and information services, where groups of professionals are responsible for serving a user group more or less directly. The close professional contact between information worker and user and between information workers should foster cooperation and a sharing of information about how best the user can be served. There should be a recognition that every participant has something to contribute and that progress and change are group activities in which all share.

Power is an important consideration when thinking about the activities of such groups. A basic definition of power might be 'the ability to achieve change'. It implies that others may share in the process of change but that they, individually or as a group, allow their own interests and concerns to be subsumed under those of a leader, for some period. It does not imply that tenancy of the position of leader is permanent or even long lasting.

The function of leadership should be carefully distinguished from the concept of titular authority: though some are labelled 'Senior Assistant' or 'Librarian-in-charge' this does not mean that they will necessarily assume, or be recognized in, the role of leader in all circumstances.

The concept of 'power bases' may be helpful here. There is much discussion in the management literature about what constitutes leadership, whether leadership skills can be taught and in what circumstances leaders may best function. Steers[4] lists several 'bases' of power which can be used to achieve compliance. The first is 'coercion': the use, or threat, of physical sanctions. This is rarely possible, and perhaps not desirable, in the working circumstances of libraries and information services.

The ability to reward through the allocation of tangible benefits such as salaries, wages and fringe benefits is another power base. Such rewards may also extend to less obvious areas such as allocation to places where working conditions are more attractive or where there may be greater possibility of engaging in activities which the recipient especially values.

'Social' or 'normative' power connotes the ability to award marks of esteem or prestige. Within a group, this is an important means of control.

To those who accept the norms of behaviour of the group, membership of the group is granted, the individual is recognized, accepted and receives response and feedback from other group members. The individual who does not accept such norms, or departs from them, risks alienation. As social animals, most people depend upon group membership and shared identification with a group or groups to foster their own sense of identity. Being cut off from this source of social gratification is very threatening to the individual and, in most cases, the aberrant behaviour quickly ceases. It can also be quite subtle in its operation: refusing to respond or laugh at another's jokes, for example, can cause considerable discomfiture. This pattern of behaviour can occur in all kinds of social group, be it work group, a group of friends sharing a meal, members of a sport club and so on.

Three other power bases are commonly recognized. The first is legitimate or authority-based power. Formally, an organization confers on someone a title; that person is ordained, or set apart, from the rest of the group and has responsibilities to the organization. The successful use of legitimate power depends on the willingness of others to recognize and respect such authority and is not, except in cultures which emphasize hierarchy and deference, a strong position from which to promote change.

'Control of resources' is another base. Most changes require the ready cooperation of workers and the use of physical resources, materials and equipment. Use can be denied or hindered, often in subtle ways. Non-cooperation through direct refusal may be inappropriate or considered rude; instead, the required resources will be deemed to be in use for other purposes, inappropriate, or otherwise not available.

Charismatic power represents the final base. Some individuals are strongly imbued with personal qualities which make them attractive to others and capable of inspiring loyalty. It is the opposite, perhaps, of the qualities of the unfortunate individual whose assessment for promotion included the memorable phrase: 'His subordinates would follow him only out of a sense of curiosity'. Charismatic power is a quality which has been displayed by some, such as leaders of religious groups, statesmen, military leaders and businessmen. It is, perhaps, not a quality which is very evident within professional circles. Since this kind of power is tenuous and so strongly dependent upon the continuing success of the individual, it is probably no bad thing that the information profession tends to rely upon qualities other than messianic zeal to achieve its ends.

Power is an intangible concept; insubstantial, difficult to define and very difficult to control. The effects of its exercise are sometimes subtle.

The publicly acknowledged power structure, usually based on authority, is one small aspect of the place the concept of power occupies in managing organizations. All managers should be aware of the overlapping, intersecting bases of power present in the culture of their organizations and should regard them not as a threat but as a natural expression of human behaviour. They must be taken into consideration when planning change but they are also one of the tools which can be used to facilitate change if the power-holders can be identified and persuaded to cooperate.

The responsibilities of consultation

It might be thought that organizational change in any organization is simply a matter of senior management determining what is best and then arranging to implement it. Except in the most authoritarian cultures, such a view is naïve. The culture of our society, modern management thinking and our professional approach dictate the need for consultation before major changes are decided upon.

A group of professional librarians and information workers is a structure quite unlike the arrangements one might find in many factories or large commercial organizations. In the latter surroundings, work is divided into stages, departments are formed and many workers have little contact with the eventual recipient of the product; there are exceptions, notably the work group method of car assembly which was developed by Saab-Scania and Volvo in the 1970s, but these are far outweighed by organizations using functional divisions. The group of librarians and information workers is more like a collective where some have 'backroom' jobs, somewhat remote from the public, whilst others have jobs which bring them into contact with users in a client relationship. Many professional librarians and information workers have a strong identification with their users and will measure any proposed change against the likely effect on those users. In such circumstances, consultation should become a natural process, drawing on the wealth of information held by the group. A hierarchy may still be quite evident: someone in a senior position will have to sanction expenditure and lead the group to implement the change but the direction of change should emerge from a process of discussion and sharing of views, information and beliefs. Increasingly, the emphasis in library and information work is towards a team or group approach, a development which is also reflected in other 'caring' professions, such as health care and social work, and in the organization of parish clergy into team ministries.

The ideal of a unanimous view of change emerging from a group whose

31

members are aware of the likely impact on users is difficult to achieve. Any change is bound to have its proponents and opponents; senior management are likely to be affected and drawn in to the debate even if they are not, themselves, on one of the sides. It is helpful to view change as a forum in which various stakeholder groups argue and debate, form alliances, threaten and seek to conciliate with each other. The notion of a new system design emerging after an episode of dialectic (that is, logical debate about the truth of opinions held by each side) is unrealistic in most circumstances: instead, the issue of change should be looked on as a vehicle for arguments about the power relationships within the organization and between the stakeholder groups.

In addition, few libraries or information services represent either a purely hierarchic or a purely democratic structure. Most represent a mixture, often of a type where the formal structure appears hierarchic, with departments and formal lines of communication, but the informal structure for the professional staff emphasizes something of a collegiate approach, where ideas are shared and power is defined more in terms of the power base of information than in terms of authority or resource control. Progress is achieved rather through seeking an accommodation with others than through appeal to higher authority.

In the previous section, authority as a power base was defined as being associated with a formal position within an organization. Katz and Kahn[5] suggest that hierarchy is associated with the division of responsibility to minimize the risk of failure. An authority structure implies the existence of a supervisory function by which supervisors guide, instruct and communicate requirements to those under their control. The supervisory function is explicit at each level of the hierarchy: thus a set of supervisors at one level will themselves come under the influence of another set at the next higher level, and so on until the top of the hierarchy is reached. The authority structure encourages a degree of specialization, so departments are formed, committed to carrying out a set of defined tasks. A supervisor thus has a power relationship with a group or groups and is subject to a power relationship defined by contact with a superior. The extent of the power relationship is defined by what it is relevant for a supervisor to seek to control. Thus, aspects of a person's social life which influence job performance (for example, dress whilst at work, attitude to users) may be recognized as being subject to a degree of control whereas behaviour outside of working hours may not be so considered. Both supervisor and supervised groups gain their sense of identity in this kind of structure from their positions as defined by the power relationship.

A consultative approach to organizational change may threaten, or appear to threaten, the authority structure of an organization. Consultation implies that those consulted will be given all necessary information for them to be able to make an informed judgement about the most beneficial path for the development of new system designs to suit their perception of the organization and its role; it also suggests that those in a senior position who are responsible for arranging the consultation will accept and evaluate such judgements. This implies a change in the relationships between a supervisor and the supervised group. The relationship now becomes one in which communication is two-way and in which the supervisor has to recognize, and respect, the distinctive competence of the supervised group to comment upon the area of work for which they are responsible. For the best kind of supervisor, one who does not rely overmuch on authority as a power base, this presents few problems. But, in circumstances where the working relationship is not quite so good, where a condition of trust does not appertain between the supervisor and the group, this recognition would be perceived as a loss of power by the supervisor. The result may be a refusal by the supervisor to set up the necessary consultative meeting and to rely, instead, on personal experience and opinion to answer questions from senior management about the desirability of features of a new design, or the establishment of meetings at which the input of information from both sides is partial and the manner guarded. Clearly, both outcomes are undesirable.

One approach to overcoming this difficulty might be to use the systems analyst to conduct such meetings. The systems analyst, being outside the authority structure, should not upset the working relationships. However, this is too simplistic a view. In some circumstances, the analyst may be perceived as an extension of management. In addition the analyst's expertise may hinder communication because participants may feel inhibited. If workers represent stakeholder groups then the analyst is also a stakeholder and thus cannot be viewed as being disinterested. Without care, the interests of stakeholders other than the analyst and senior management may be ignored or not even recognized.

It is also possible for a stakeholder group so to dominate proceedings that the ideas of the group gain ascendancy even though they may not be as good or effective as those of another group. Rational debate may be replaced by strategies such as bargaining, covert threats and the release or concealment of important information.

Stakeholders may also take the view that they are the subjects of manipulation by senior management. This view takes as its premise the existence of a solution which senior management have already accepted and to which they are committed but the existence of which they have not revealed. The purpose of consultation is then seen to be to provide a forum for selling the solution rather than informing participants of the options and seeking reasoned response. Any volunteered information which seems to strengthen the management case will be welcomed but information critical of the case will be rejected or explained away. The stakeholder group will feel that it is responding to a hidden agenda and is being manipulated in order to give justification to the management plan. Bearing such beliefs, the group may become increasingly uncooperative or may simply decide to put up only a token show of resistance to being led in the direction indicated by management. It is important to recognize that there need not, in any objective sense, be a management plan already in existence. It is enough for the stakeholder group to believe that it is being manipulated for the responses to become dishonest or, at best, for there to be a cynical acceptance of the management plan by the group.

Consultation also implies that management will be willing to modify its views. This may be far from easy especially if the project has already gained their interest and support. When considering the response to a long-cherished plan it is tempting to rationalize criticism and become convinced that critics do not understand the plans.

So far, it has been assumed that consultation is desirable whatever the circumstances. This assumption needs consideration.

In examining the range of work which might be undertaken by a manager, it is clear that a distinction can be drawn between making decisions about matters which are urgent and those which are not. The day-to-day administration of a library or information service will require many urgent decisions and it would be unrealistic to suppose that full consultation could ever be contemplated before making such decisions. Provided the manager is aware of any relevant information, has experience of similar situations and is confident in that experience, there is no reason to suppose that the outcome will not be a feasible solution arrived at in a comparatively short time. There may be an advantage in making some decisions in this way: one person, considering all the evidence, may be able to discern and concentrate on the salient points and set aside other matters. A better decision may emerge because of this ability to focus on the problem.

The individuals in a group considering the same problem will bring

34

a range of information and opinion which will need to be shared and then evaluated so that some judgement about the importance of each item can be made. Members may need to be convinced because their own beliefs and experience may be contradicted by others. Various strategies may be used by the group to resolve differences but, in most circumstances, the group will adopt a satisficing approach: that is, a group view will emerge which minimizes the differences between members. The need to establish truth may give way to the need to keep the group intact. This strategy is rarely acknowledged openly; instead, a selective view of the evidence will be constructed by the group in an effort to rationalize its decision. The decision which eventually emerges from group discussion will be one with which most, if not all, of the members can agree but it may not be the best, when compared with a dispassionate review of the evidence, and it may take a long time to appear.

'Group think' is a term which has been applied disparagingly to the outcome of such meetings. It is unfair, though, to reject group approaches to some issues simply on the grounds that the solutions cause the minimum of upset to participants. What a manager must consider at every point where a decision is needed is whether the impact of the decision is likely to be confined to one person or one part of a process, or whether it is likely to have a wider impact. In the latter case, a group decision may be more persuasive and may help commitment to change to be built more quickly than if the decision is solely the product of one mind.

Balance theory, first propounded by Heider,[6] is a useful means of considering and explaining how a group tends to operate. Kotler and Andreasen[7] explain that a fundamental assumption of balance theory is that individuals like to have an equilibrium in their system of values, beliefs and understanding. When confronted with some piece of information which does not seem to fit or contradicts notions already present in their minds, their response is to try to restore balance. How hard and sustained that attempt is depends on the degree of imbalance and the perceived importance of the information.

For an indication of how the balance theory might explain group behaviour, consider Figure 8. Here a source (S) is represented as giving some information to a group (G) about some object of common interest (O). The source might be another group or an individual; the object of interest might be a fact, an aspect of behaviour, a plan, an individual, or whatever. The attitude of the group towards the source is represented by an algebraic operator, either a plus or minus sign, to represent a positive or negative attitude. Similarly, the group attitude towards the

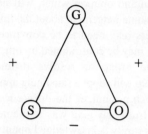

Figure 8 Balance theory

object of interest is either positive or negative, as is the attitude which the group perceives the source to have towards the object. Balance theory suggests that the system is in balance whenever the combination of algebraic signs, through multiplication, becomes positive. Thus, three plus signs represent balance, as do two minus signs and a plus (minus multiplied by minus yields plus and plus multiplied by plus yields plus). The remaining possible combinations of three minus signs or two plus signs and a minus indicate a system which is out of balance. If the system is out of balance, the group will adjust its perceptions in an attempt to restore equilibrium.

Consider an example. Suppose an individual (the source) is presenting a scheme (the object) for the introduction of fees for conducting online searches. If the starting position of the group is broadly in favour of the scheme, but it is perceived that the source is not, the group response will depend on its attitude towards the source. If the attitude is positive then the system will be out of balance. There are four possible responses.

The first possibility is that the group may change its attitude towards the scheme: in other words the personality of, or respect for, the source may be strong enough to induce the group to change its view of the desirability of the scheme.

In the second case, the group may change its attitude towards the source. This implies that the group is very firmly convinced of the correctness of its view of the object and this is sufficient for its positive view of the source to be replaced by a negative, critical, view.

A third possibility is that the group distorts its perception of what the source has said. This means that the group imputes additional, undisclosed, motives to the source for presenting arguments against the scheme and concludes that the source is really in favour of it.

The final possibility is that the group decides to reduce the perceived importance of the issue to a point where it can live with the residual tension created by the imbalance.

Clearly, the first possibility is desirable if the intent of management is to persuade a group of the need for change. The choice of source will be crucial.

The role of the systems analyst

The team approach to management has been widely adopted in libraries and information services; even in small-scale services the sharing of managerial decision-making is recognized as desirable because it enables expertise to be shared and encourages commitment. In conducting the analysis of a system, team work is vital if the necessary information is to be collected quickly and without disruption and if full understanding of the findings is to be fostered. Someone has to take on the role of analyst, a key position, and one of considerable power. It is especially important, therefore, that the person selected has the right qualities for the job.

The ideal is to have someone from outside the organization: a consultant who has no obvious axe to grind, no departmental sensibilities to protect. Such a person will be able to give an objective view of the system, its good and bad points, and the opportunities for development and change. Good analysts will be able to call upon a body of experience, both their own and the corpus of professional knowledge to which they have access; they will be able to import new ideas into the service. Sometimes, however, this may be a focus for trouble. It all too easy to dismiss such imports as unlikely to be suitable: 'it wasn't invented here' is often the underlying theme of objections to new ideas. The need for a sensitive and confident approach by the analyst is vital. An outside consultant is rarely able to enforce change: the consultant is only able to influence the direction and progress of change. In other words, the power base of the outside consultant is information and change will only come about if this power is allied to the power of people in key positions within the organization. Such individuals or groups have to be convinced that the direction and pace of change proposed *is* consonant with the objectives of the organization and will meet the needs of users. Only then can they begin to lead the rest of the staff to accept change.

It is rarely possible to justify employing an outside consultant for anything other than very large or sensitive projects. Usually, someone already on the staff must be selected to take the role for the duration of the project. It is possible to divide the role up and allocate parts of it to a number of people but coordination of the work may then become very difficult, especially if the system being investigated is complex. Another approach is to appoint a small group: the appointment of a team leader with responsibilities and authority for management of the team and coordination of the investigation is important.

Having the analysis conducted by an in-house person or team has an additional value: if the systems approach to planning is to be used again there will always be a need for someone with analytic skills to hand, responsible for monitoring, testing and investigating. This may not necessarily be a full-time role, but the cumulation of experience, the cast of mind and the development of the approach will be valuable attributes which can also enhance other roles. The trend in many areas of management, notably of libraries and information services, has been to develop permanent, or semi-permanent, project teams often based on a 'matrix' view of the organization and managerial responsibilities. As well as functional, 'line', responsibilities, each manager has an overview of some area of development and is responsible for alerting the group to interesting ideas or emerging possibilities. The placing of an analyst in a team is helpful if ideas are to be developed from the conceptual stage to reality.

In choosing a person for the job of analyst it should be borne in mind that the person conducting the analysis is not just using a set of techniques, but is involved in the process of change. The analyst is often viewed as an agent of change and may thus be resisted or welcomed depending on how those being investigated view the desirability of change. Although change represents a normal and healthy state for a system it also presents many problems, most of them related to human behaviour. The analyst needs to be sensitive to such problems, but not overawed by them. Similarly, it is necessary for managers to be aware that the focus of interest of the analyst should include some consideration of human and social factors, as well as a study of technical factors.

What qualities should one look for in a systems analyst? The following list of personal qualities is an ideal: it is unlikely that someone with all will be found, but it isolates those areas of character which should be fairly strongly represented.

Perception is a key quality: in analysing any task it will be necessary to link the information given to that given by other people. Imagination may be needed to perceive the relationship between a piece of information supplied by one person and that given by another. Odd scraps of information may be collected during the course of the investigation. It may be some time before they can be fitted into the general picture but the analyst must remember them and be able to see, at the appropriate time, how they may be used to complete the picture.

It is rare that all the information can be gathered in an orderly fashion and the information may be incomplete: the analyst must persist in questioning and observing until the loose ends have been discovered and tied into the general picture. This calls for stamina!

Strength of character may seem to be an odd trait to expect. It is included because the analyst is expected to be objective and not to take sides. Those being analysed may think otherwise and try to press the analyst into acting as their channel of communication to the management. Being in the middle in such circumstances is uncomfortable and should certainly be avoided if the clear analytic view is to be preserved. This is one point on which the internally appointed analyst may be at some disadvantage: loyalties built up through working with others in the organization may be difficult to surmount and a proper sense of objectivity may be difficult to sustain. Conversely, a person placed in this position may respond by behaving in an aloof manner and not, seemingly, be willing to respond to the legitimate concerns of fellow-workers. Either response is unhelpful and will result in distortions. It will be difficult for the internally appointed person to avoid either extreme: for management, this consideration reinforces the need to select the person with care, to pay careful attention to the need for training and to recognize the mental strain under which an analyst may be forced to work.

Breadth of outlook is concerned with the ability to remain interested in whatever level of work the analyst is observing. It may be very exciting to analyse the work of senior management but the work of others lower down the hierarchy should not then be looked upon as tedious and not worth the effort of full analysis. Work, at all levels, contributes to the overall success of any enterprise; it is especially the case in library and information services that the public image depends largely on the work of library assistants and those close to the users.

Orderliness and discipline are key qualities: analysis creates a lot of information, which will need to be organized. This is not a rewarding task, but the analyst has to be a paragon in this respect. Spotting loose ends is only possible if the recording system in use draws them to the attention of the analyst. This means creating orderly files and using a standard method of documentation for recording the results of interviews, questionnaires and observation. It also relies upon the earlier-mentioned quality of perception to link all this material together. Discipline is necessary if the result of a hard day's interviewing or observation is to be documented. Leaving it until tomorrow may result in the loss of a fleeting impression or small clue which can lead the alert analyst to a significant, but hitherto unrecorded, fact. The analyst's day needs to be carefully organized to allow adequate time for recording, administration and thought.

During the task of investigation, the analyst will encounter people of very different character, levels of education, degrees of responsibility and so on. These people must be persuaded to cooperate, whatever their state of mind or position in the organization. Some may be very defensive: 'I've done this job for years. Are you suggesting I don't know what's best?' Others may be seeking an ally: 'Perhaps I shouldn't tell you this, but . . .' Some may need encouragement since they may not believe that their jobs are important or that anyone could be interested in the details. Some may need no encouragement to talk: the analyst may have to steer the conversation discreetly back to the matter in hand. The analyst must not only be interested in what is being said but must also convince the other person that the conversation is interesting. Momentary inattention or faint signs of boredom are enough to reduce people to silence and to foster non-cooperation. Equally, it is easy to create distrust and dislike by appearing to talk down to people or by making assumptions about their work. The problem may be exacerbated for the internally appointed analyst by the power structure of the organization. If the analyst occupies a higher or lower position in the organization, relative to the person being interviewed, trust may be an important issue. This may be especially true in an organization where the power structure emphasizes hierarchy, status and position but less so where a collegiate atmosphere prevails. The function of the analyst is to create conditions in which people feel comfortable and able to talk about their work. High social skill is one of the most important characteristics of the good analyst.

Terms of reference
When appointing an analyst from outside the organization it is normal to prepare terms of reference for the project. These provide an agreed statement about the duties, responsibilities and behaviour of the analyst.

It is much less common for terms of reference to be prepared for internally appointed analysts: somehow custom and practice, good sense and an awareness of responsibility are expected to take the place of formal statements. This is unfortunate because if there are questions about the conduct of the analysis, behaviour of the analyst, duties and responsibilities, there is nothing tangible to which reference may be made. It is also unfair to the analyst who will be occupying a demanding role within the organization. A formal statement may offer guidance in moments of uncertainty and may provide some authoritative backing in the event of disputes.

Such statements can have additional roles if they are made known within the organization. First, they will act as an introduction to the idea of systems analysis and help to define the role of the analyst. Secondly, they will outline the scope of the work to be undertaken. It is especially important that staff are aware of survey arrangements: does the analyst have permission to approach them directly and arrange appointments for interviews or must the analyst first seek permission from a departmental head? Some of the information which may be elicited could be confidential or critical of those in authority and staff may need reassurance about how the information is to be used.

It is best to prepare written, agreed, statements outlining:

- *scope* of the investigation (what parts of the system, processes, departments, personnel, products will be studied);
- *objectives* (what problem or opportunity is being explored; what questions the analysis will aim to answer);
- *constraints* (areas, topics, problems and people considered to be excluded from the investigation; time allowed for the investigation; financial constraints);
- *resources available* (people, facilities);
- *conduct* (procedures for seeking permission to observe, question or interview staff and others; procedures for reporting findings; responsibilities for use of resources).

For an investigation employing outside appointment of consultants these details will need careful and extensive consideration. For the small-scale, in-house job there is a temptation not to define matters too closely, relying on good sense and day-to-day contact to clarify any misunderstandings: this can work quite well, but *some* terms of reference need to be agreed otherwise the analyst may find it difficult to decide when to finish the investigation and move on to producing the feasibility report.

What the analyst must remember
In dealing with any organization the analyst must recognize that most are complex structures which have evolved over a considerable period of time and continue to evolve. They are also complex mixtures of people,

structures and expectations loosely bound together by some common purpose. The background of the organization and its human aspects constitute two major areas which the analyst must consider.

In discussing the background of an organization the analyst must remember that the systems which have evolved represent its structure and purpose. Such systems do not necessarily reflect stated objectives: the objective of most organizations, once set up, is to survive but few would openly lay claim to this as their purpose. Instead, a statement of mission will represent the function of the organization to the public. The analyst may discover many curiosities of arrangement and administration, some of which may be difficult to link with the mission statement. This is often the case in organizations with long histories or those which have evolved quickly: structures and processes may be retained long after their usefulness is exhausted, simply because no one has questioned their continuance. The analyst should not worry at this: it is something to be noted for further discussion.

Systems are devised and are then influenced by the people who have to work with them. It is a common finding that a system designed now will, in six months' time, have been changed subtly by workers. The most stringent rules and procedures can be established, intensive training can be given and yet, in some small respect, each of us will adapt any task which we are given. It is an expression of individualism, an opportunity to exercise a little autonomy, a chance to remind ourselves that we matter. Once again, the analyst should not be surprised if procedures laid down in staff manuals are not followed completely or accurately. What is important is for the analyst to discover what *is* being done and to assess how efficiently and effectively it is being done.

Organizations are a mixture of formal and informal systems. The analyst may first discover the formal system enshrined in an organization chart, procedures manual or summary description of objectives. These present a picture of the divisions, departments and hierarchies. They will lay down the routes for reports and outline the authority structure but will not show the way in which the organization, considered as a set of social groups, really operates.

The 'grapevine' is a familiar example of the informal communication structure which operates in all organizations: everyone who has been accepted as part of a group is plugged in to the grapevine and sends and receives information, rumour and misinformation. The network of relationships represented by the grapevine is not reflected in the formal organization chart. A senior manager may find that a colleague at a lower managerial level or in another department is the point of contact. The jest that 'if something's going on the janitors are the first to know' has a ring of truth about it and certainly reflects the power of the grapevine. The 'gatekeeper' concept, often exploited in setting up current awareness services, is another manifestation of the notion that certain people in an organization are key collection and distribution points for information. Inform them and, quite quickly, almost everyone will know.

The grapevine is one example of an informal system. Others can be seen if the pattern of working relationships is observed. The most important, from the point of view of the analyst, are work groups. These are formed of employees, often in the same department or carrying out similar tasks. Norms concerning rate of work, starting and finishing times, problem-solving and general behaviour are quickly established and a group leader often emerges. Some behaviour may stretch or defy the formal rules of the organization, though often in fairly trivial ways: taking 20 minutes instead of 15 for a coffee-break, for example. On the other hand, such groups can support members experiencing difficulties or having 'off' days. They can also discipline members whose rate of work is, for no good reason, less than the group norm. Groups thus provide a form of control which members are willing to accept in return for the social benefits and closeness which such structures afford. Most people, with the possible exception of sociopaths, prefer the company of others and will seek to be accepted by a group.

Group membership extends throughout the hierarchy of the organization: there will be work groups at senior management level as well as amongst clerical assistants and middle-management. Some work groups may have a life outside the internal environment, reflected, perhaps, in common membership of a club or the pursuance of a leisure activity. This sharing of work and other activities encourages the formation of strong bonds of loyalty which individuals will be unwilling to transgress for fear of the disapproval of the group. Leadership may be shared, the particular skill or knowledge needed at the time being the deciding factor in the choice of leader at a particular moment. In many cases someone emerges as leader, perhaps the person who normally initiates activities.

Groups commonly allocate roles to members. 'Leader' is one such role; others are 'facilitator', the person who tries to organize resources so that things are done; 'conciliator', who tries to bring about agreement where there is conflict; 'shaper', who tries to mould ideas from the group; 'jester', the person who can be relied upon to break an awkward moment with a joke, and so on.

Why should a consideration of such matters be important to the systems analyst? Consider the problem of implementing a new system. It is quite likely that working relationships will be altered by its introduction. Some groups will be split up, and some individuals will find themselves working with members of other groups. There will be an alteration in the power relationships between individuals and between groups. A large group, perceived as powerful by other groups, may be split. Its power will be seen as diminished whilst another group may be seen as having gained power through increased membership or the accession to membership of particular individuals. This will disturb groups and individuals who perceive themselves as losing power. The change to group membership and the change to the power structure will be resisted and a period of conflict will ensue.

The acute analyst will recognize the likelihood of this occurrence and plan for its management, if it cannot be avoided. Sensitive design of processes and the internal environment can reduce the incidence of outbreaks of conflict but complete avoidance is too much to expect. The best that can be done is to alleviate the effects and to facilitate the development of new groupings and new norms of behaviour as soon as possible. During the process of investigation of the system the analyst must be alert to the need to discern what groups exist and how they are organized. In particular, a knowledge of which workers are regarded as group leaders can be very useful when trying to promote change. Discussion with leaders can often prove helpful in spotting problems in existing processes and new designs and for reducing the potential for conflict.

It is also helpful at the start of an analysis to spend some time in gathering information about the history, present and past objectives and anticipated future of the organization. A consideration of these statements will reveal what the members of the organization *think* it is doing and how they like to think the organization is perceived by users and society in general. It is rare to find that these expectations are borne out by the analysis. The Hillingdon study[8] for example, revealed many apparent misapprehensions by members of the public about the library service, its facilities and ambience. But, were these mistaken views or evidence of a mismatch between the perception of the library service as held by the staff and that held by those outside? Only a careful investigation of the services offered and how well these met the needs of users and potential users could reveal which is true. In any case, the fact that some people perceive the library service in unfavourable terms *is* important. Analysis may also reveal that a belief that the organization is carrying out some function cannot be supported by evidence. For example, a company information service manager may believe that some of the needs of the marketing department are being met by circulating details of products made by competitors. If no one in the marketing department follows up such information, or if it is obtained more quickly from elsewhere, the information service manager would be foolish to continue to assume that this aspect of the service was successful. It is often the painful task of the analyst to draw attention to the differences between belief, expectation and actual performance.

Systems theory suggests that all organizations exist within an environment consisting of the rules and conventions of society, laws, stakeholder groups, and physical, economic and other factors. Figure 6 (page 23) illustrates this. The 'general' environment can be distinguished from the 'operating' environment which may be thought of as being constituted of rules, stakeholder groups, such as suppliers and users, and physical, economic and other factors. An organization also has an 'internal' environment — the procedures and groups, such as staff, which constitute the system. The general and operating environments may provide opportunities for growth, development and change but the characteristics of both may curtail or circumscribe what it is possible to do. For example, a company information service may be permitted by the managing director to reorganize its facilities to provide a more effective service subject to the constraint that the running costs remain the same: the operating environment sanctions change in one direction but subjects it to control through an economic factor.

The internal environment might, in the same example, put a brake on change because of some limitation in the availability of resources. If the proposed changes require staff to be trained in skills such as wordprocessing the change cannot take place until this is achieved.

The constraints on, and opportunities for, growth presented by the general environment are long term and reflect changes in the social and cultural life of a society or country. The gradual shift from rate-supported, supposedly 'free' services to direct charging is a response by the operating environment to economic and legislative changes within the general environment. It is usually very difficult to recognize, record and assess such changes early in their development because their evolution depends so much on public and political debate followed by government action. For service organizations, the best approach is for the management to be aware of the political process and to be prepared to consider the implications of the arguments presented in such debates as may be evident: when the operating environment is subject to change, it will not come as a complete surprise. The essence of success is the ability to anticipate the need to respond strategically rather than reacting to a stimulus.

This is not to suggest that managers should neglect opportunities to influence the general environment but it is a suggestion that bringing about social and political changes are long-term activities, involving professional attitudes and beliefs, rather than the short- to medium-term activities which comprise resource management.

The tasks of the systems analyst are to seek out the factors in the operating and internal environments which control or circumscribe change and to consider what effect such control might have on any proposals. The aim is to identify the difference between what facilities are needed for a successful change and those which are available. Once identified, the management of the organization can consider whether the environments can be influenced in some way to make the acquisition of the necessary facilities feasible. Sometimes a complete solution can be realized, sometimes only partial achievement is rendered possible: it is for the analyst to guide management into thinking about the problem.

The discussion has centred on the characteristics of the organization. People, too, will exhibit certain characteristics which the analyst must consider when undertaking any kind of study.

A new recruit to an organization comes with a set of beliefs and attitudes formed by experience, contact with family and friends, and the surrounding culture. The first days within the organization are a process of socialization, during which the new recruit is exposed to the values, attitudes and beliefs of those already in the organization and to statements about its role and functions. In turn, those in contact with the new recruit are affected by the 'mind set' of the recruit. This process of accommodation and acclimatization can best be considered as 'establishing a psychological contract'. Such mental contracts complement formal, written, contracts of employment in that they summarize a set of beliefs and expectations about the organization and work within it. If, for example, the recruit observes that up to five minutes late arrival is not remarked upon then the belief that such behaviour is ignored will form part of the contract. The stated organizational objectives of a public library might indicate that its purpose is to serve the information needs of all members of the surrounding community but the actual experience of the recruit might be that certain sections of that community are favoured. Thus, a set of attitudes and beliefs about work and the organization are formed.

A major problem arises when different sets of attitudes and beliefs are held by various groups. This is almost inevitable because the daily experiences of a library assistant, for example, are different from those of the manager of the library service. Each encounters a distinct range of people, problems and opportunities and each has a range of ways of responding. It is unlikely that the range of experience, and the beliefs, of the two will concur. Each will have different expectations about work. The analyst must be aware of this and must be able to convey this sense of difference when discussing the findings of a study.

Consider library automation. A senior manager may see this as offering a more effective control of resources, better service to users and more amenable jobs for assistants. Surely, no one would object? The assistant working on the issue desk may see it as an imposition which will break up satisfying working relationships and replace a variety of manual routines with one invariant routine in which all skill has been replaced by the boring activity of scanning bar-coded labels with a light-pen. The senior manager may have a unitary view of the the library, in which everyone is 'just part of one big, happy, ship'; the assistant may see it, instead, as being a set of rowing boats all facing in different directions. If automation is to be introduced without too much disturbance and dispute some accommodation between the views has to be reached and the starting point for this is the recognition, at the outset, that different opinions are held. The analyst is in the best position to be aware of such differences.

Resistance to change is a fact of organizational life. It will impinge upon the work of the analyst in several ways. The initial stages of the study of an organization are based on discussion, interviews and observation. The success of each depends on cooperation: willingness to engage in the study and not to mislead or to withhold information. Sabotage need not be an overt act: a strongly defensive attitude may be enough to prevent a free flow of ideas and thus prejudice the outcome of the investigation. Later stages may depend on willingness to learn new, or modified, techniques. Successful learning depends on the self-motivation of the trainee. Resistance to change will hinder the development of this self-motivation. The success of the design of a modified process may depend on the response of users to a model or prototype: resistance to change may lead users to withhold or suppress critical comment or to engage in destructive criticism. In each case, true responses are coloured by resistance to change.

The task of the analyst is to anticipate such resistance and to be prepared to allow the feelings engendered by it to be expressed as openly as possible. Only when they have had a good airing, been formally acknowledged, and any misconceptions recognized and corrected, can the development of more positive attitudes be assisted.

Almost as serious is an uncritical enthusiasm for change. This usually results from unrealistic expectations about the transformation of working life by, for example, the use of new technology. A justification for introducing computer-assisted systems is their ability to replace the so-called drudgery of work with a manual system. A rosy picture of a future free from tedious tasks is painted for the benefit of library staff. It is true that the nature of the process is changed but many assistants would question whether the quality of their working life is materially improved. This is not to suggest that those responsible for the design and implementation of the new systems are mendacious: rather, it is a case of inexperience and an unwillingness to assess critically the experience of others engaged in similar projects. The analyst has an important role in keeping management and users in touch with reality, which often means explaining that the new system *will* have problems though they may be different from those experienced with the previous system.

It is also important for managers to realize that improvements to one part of a system may simply move a problem to another part. Solving the acquisitions department bottleneck may increase the cataloguing department backlog unless some attention is given to balancing the workflow in both departments, for example. An over-enthusiasm for change can lead to concentration on one part of a system to the detriment of other parts and, ultimately, the whole system.

Being perceived as an agent of change can make the analyst vulnerable to the attentions of those having some wish to alter the power relationships within the organization. Such people may seek to use the analyst as a tool, or channel of communication, to spread ideas and discontent and to seek to consolidate their own position within the organization. The analyst has the difficult task of gaining their cooperation without becoming party to a conspiracy.

There may be problems originating from the senior management level as well. This may arise from commitment to an idea or proposed new system. A strong identification with a project may lead senior management to assume that their enthusiasm and commitment is shared by others. It may frequently be necessary for the analyst to remind the senior management that the implementation of new ideas should be viewed as a process which involves many stakeholders all of whom will need to be informed and involved. It is also important that the sense of a project being someone's 'baby' or personal idea is abandoned early on. Neglecting to facilitate this 'letting go' will result in the 'owner' of the project becoming defensive in the face of legitimate criticism and this will stifle improvement and development.

Facilitating consultation

The process of consultation is of critical importance to the sound development of a project. The responsibility for establishing circumstances which facilitate the process is shared between management and the analyst. If the analyst is already in a senior position within the management structure then it may be supposed that this task will be easy because groups can be summoned and discussions initiated almost at will but a consideration of power relationships and the process of consultation should warn against any such supposition. It is certainly possible to summon groups, explain the circumstances and reasons for the meeting and then invite comment. It is most unlikely that much will be elicited and what is given will probably reflect the group's perception of what it is the manager wants to hear.

The analyst lower down the management structure of the organization has an easier task when dealing with those at the same level but may have to cope with defensive behaviour when dealing with those above or below in the hierarchy.

The analyst from outside the organization is often best able to facilitate consultation, for several reasons. Such a person has novelty value: a new face, and an evident willingness to listen, will often encourage groups and individuals to be open and ready to discuss. The outsider may be perceived as having no 'axe to grind', no link with the established power structure. Because the outsider lacks the detailed historical knowledge of the organization which can only come from having worked for it for some time, each point or suggestion which is made will need to be explained and its context outlined. Essentially, the advantage is one of encouraging flow of conversation: the difficulty is in starting the flow. The need to explain will provides a conversational 'ball' which can be exchanged between the analyst and the group.

Whatever the managerial position and status of the analyst, the major problem in facilitating a free exchange of ideas and opinions is in being

49

perceived as a tool of management. The first steps that management can take to reduce this appearance is in the establishment and promulgation of the terms of reference of the analyst. A clear statement of purpose, intent and methods of procedure will encourage the view that project development is to be conducted openly.

The ideal is to have already the kind of organizational culture which assumes consultation will take place and that the views of all are welcome and important. Many libraries and information services tend not to have strongly hierarchic management structures: the conditions are good, therefore, for the encouragement of consultative processes.

How should this be fostered? The first step is essential: senior management must accept that group relationships and the processes of discussion are important areas for the development of the organization. Secondly, the process of learning should be structured around a problem though it need not, initially, be clearly defined. Thirdly, the process should involve all levels in the organization: in this way, the new culture is seen to affect everyone and will not be perceived as a sop to those lower down the structure.

Assume that it has been agreed to call a consultative meeting of senior staff to discuss an apparent problem with training. Ideally, participants will have been selected who are stakeholders and thus have some particular interest in the problem. Since the problem is, at present, ill-defined this may include many people.

The purpose of a first, or exploratory, meeting is to determine more precisely what the problem is perceived to be: that is, how does each member of the group see the problem and in what respects do these views differ? It is important that the analyst should not dominate the meeting or seek to lead discussion. Instead, the analyst should invite the principal stakeholder, who is usually the person who first identified the problem, to state briefly what the problem appears to be. Thereafter, the analyst should ask questions which seek to sharpen the problem statement and should invite other participants to make similar statements of the problem as seen by them. A helpful technique is to ask each participant in turn to present a brief statement and to suppress, for the moment, reactions to the statements of others. This facilitates a flow of comment and encourages involvement.

Another important condition at this point in the process is to discourage evaluation: in this respect, the technique has something in common with 'brainstorming'. Evaluation of ideas is essential before action is taken but at this stage it is rarely helpful and will certainly discourage others.

It is important to realize that approving of something is as evaluative a comment as disapproving of it. Both positive and negative comments should be discouraged.

The second stage of the consultative process is concerned with testing how open the participants are prepared to be. The analyst should be aware of attempts at concealing motives, of confusion over the role of the analyst and an unwillingness to proceed with discussions. Nothing fruitful will be achieved until the existence of these feelings has been acknowledged. The analyst is not there in the role of expert problem-solver and this should be made clear early on in the meeting. One of the dangers of the role of analyst is being perceived as the 'expert': the analyst may be seduced into discussing the problem in some depth and will thus begin to 'own' it and think about its solution. This kind of identification is to be avoided: whatever solutions are to emerge should come from the group and the role of the analyst is to facilitate its development.

The analyst must avoid the appearance of aloofness: trust is a vital component in the relationship and will only be built up if the analyst is willing to engage in the discussion. Response from the analyst is important but that response does not need to be evaluative. Rather, it should aim to encourage discussion.

Reflective questioning is often helpful, especially if the analyst senses that an important fact, opinion or feeling has been hinted at but not openly stated. The technique is simple: the analyst reflects the comments of a participant, thus passing the 'ball' back. For example:

Participant:'The staff are not very happy with the present system.'
Analyst: 'The staff are not very happy?'
Participant:'Yes, its mainly the issue desk staff — they say there is a problem there.'
Analyst: 'There's a problem with the issue desk?'

and so on. This technique is non-invasive: it uses the information which the respondent has offered, information about which the participant is confident and willing to divulge, and it encourages a flow of conversation and the creation of a sense of trust — provided it is not carried to extremes.

Another useful approach is for the analyst to summarize the points which have emerged but using the analyst's words. Quite often, this will elicit the comment: 'That's not quite what I meant . . .' Once again, flow of conversation has been encouraged, a misapprehension may be corrected, and some additional information may emerge.

As confidence in the relationship grows, the analyst can ask more probing questions, such as: 'What did you mean by ...?' or 'Why do you believe ... to be true?' It is important, though, to remain aware of the behaviour of the participants: any sense of unease or unwillingness to answer indicates the need to revert to a less invasive approach.

The analyst is also in a good position to observe the process of group discussion: who talks to whom, whose comments tend to be ignored and who introduces new ideas. In this way, some appreciation of the power structure within the group can be formed. Non-verbal behaviour may also provide a valuable clue to the level of involvement of each participant. Signs of boredom, avoiding eye contact with the group, extensive doodling, may indicate someone who has yet to build up sufficient trust to be committed to the process of consultation. The analyst may have to guide conversation so that the person is more directly involved or, if this is not successful, may better discuss matters in private with the individual. It is important to ensure that apparent indifference is not ignored because it can be used to cloak a much deeper-seated unease about the consequences of whatever project the organization has in mind.

Part of the process of communication is the giving and receiving of feedback. In the first stages of the consultative process, much of the analyst's work will be concerned with facilitating the flow of conversation and ideas but the time will come when the participants will ask the analyst to respond to them: in essence, the question is 'How do we seem to you?' What is not required at this point is a discussion of the ideas which have been presented but, instead, feedback on how the group behaviour is perceived by the analyst. The request will only come when an atmosphere of trust has been engendered but if people are not yet ready to hear something the result may be that the accuracy of the feedback is challenged or the views presented by the analyst may be distorted and rejected. What the analyst chooses to comment on will depend upon experience and how well the participants and analyst know each other.

In the initial stages of consultation, it is best to confine feedback to areas concerned with the way in which the group is working rather than comment on individuals. Comments on the following areas should be beneficial:

- Is there a group leader or leaders and what functions are they fulfilling?
- What rules, if any, pertain to making decisions?

- How are decisions taken: by majority, unanimity, consensus, or by high-status members?
- Do people stray from the topic under discussion?
- How is time allocated?

At later stages, when participants and analyst feel more secure in their relationship, the comments can go deeper:

- How is progress reviewed and how frequently?
- Is the group willing to allow unstructured discussion when creative thought is needed?
- Are people engaged in the discussion or coasting, creating diversions and playing about?
- Are the talents of each person being used?
- How effective is the group at organizing itself and its work?

Some comment on individuals may also be helpful:

- How often does each participant speak; are there interruptions from other participants; what attempts does each participant make to involve others?
- Do people listen to each other; who is ignored?
- Do people seem committed to decisions?
- What power structure or hierarchy is evident; what alliances have been formed?
- Is the atmosphere friendly, supportive and cooperative?
- How are disagreements and disputes settled?

The purpose of providing feedback is to enable the group to work more satisfactorily because participants will begin to understand the effect of their behaviour, collectively and individually, on each other. The positive as well as the negative aspects need to be mentioned. Feedback is a vital part of learning to function as a group.

The early stages of group building are important if a group is to cohere and carry out useful work. Running libraries and information services needs a variety of skills and one of the best arenas for appreciating the range available is through a team approach to managing change.

Notes

1   Weber, M., *The theory of social and economic organization*, New York, Oxford University Press, 1947.

2   Mayo, E., *The social problems of an industrial civilisation*, London, Routledge, 1949.

3   Likert, R., *New patterns of management*, New York, McGraw Hill, 1961.

4   Steers, R. M., *Introduction to organizational behavior*, 2nd ed., Glenview, Scott, Foresman, 1984, 309-10.

5   Katz, D. and Kahn, R. L., *The social psychology of organizations*, 2nd ed., New York, Wiley, 1978, 323.

6   Heider, F., 'Attitudes and cognitive organizations', *Journal of psychology*, **21**, 1946, 107-12.

7   Kotler, P. and Andreasen, A. R., *Strategic marketing for nonprofit organizations*, 3rd ed., Englewood Cliffs, New Jersey, Prentice-Hall, 1987, 528-9.

8   Totterdell, B. and Bird, J., *The effective library: report of the Hillingdon project on public library effectiveness*, London, Library Association, 1976.

3 *What needs to be studied?*

Problems and opportunities

It is a sad fact that problems tend to dominate life, sometimes to the extent that it becomes difficult to see that there are also many opportunities. Managerial life is no exception to this dictum and there is a danger that many managers will spend the majority of their time in reacting to problems rather than seeking to improve their organizations and the services offered through the taking of opportunities.

Opportunities and problems are opposite sides of the same coin, it is said, and there is truth in this. A problem represents a deficiency of some kind, a mismatch between expectation and performance. In solving the problem it may be possible to extend the solution to provide improvements. The taking of opportunities suggests seeking to develop something beyond the bounds of what is currently being done. In this sense the aphorism is too restricted to represent the ethos of management. The successful manager must be both a problem-solver and an active explorer of possibilities for development of the organization: the manager must be aware of the needs of the market and able to judge how well the organization can meet those needs.

A project can be started as a result of the recognition of a problem or the perception that there is an opportunity to explore. Unfortunately, problems and opportunities rarely present themselves clearly and unequivocally. What may be a problem to one group of people is perceived quite differently by another. The designated problem may be perceived as a symptom of a much more severe disease affecting many parts of an organization. Thus, there may be disagreement on the extent and likely effect of a problem; there may be disagreement on the attractiveness of an opportunity. What is needed, before resources are committed to further study, is a limited exploration by senior management to try to recognize and agree on the nature of the problem or opportunity.

55

The systems analyst can assist in this process but should beware of becoming anything more than a facilitator at this stage. Eden[1] has made a useful distinction between styles of help, calling them 'coercive', 'empathetic' and 'negotiative'.

The coercive style is evident when the analyst begins to redefine a problem, often by offering to simplify and clarify the issues. The apparent help has the effect of promoting the position of power of the analyst by turning a problem which the analyst does not initially understand into something familiar. The attempt is rarely crude or obvious; it may, indeed, be encouraged by a group wishing for an 'objective' view. It is also possible that the analyst may be unaware that this style is developing: the problem is that most of us, when confronted with something new, tend to try to perceive it in terms of things we already know and with which we have already worked. At this stage in the life of a project it is vital that the group be encouraged to own and explore the problem or opportunity and resist the temptation to tidy up its presentation.

The empathetic style aims at encouraging the group to explore the problem or opportunity: the analyst uses the reflective technique, outlined in chapter 2, and is careful to avoid suggesting aspects of the problem or delving beyond the point at which the group is comfortable. The analyst seeks to understand the problem or opportunity as it seems from the point of view of the group. This may become difficult, because each member will have a different view and, in attempting to resolve these differences, the analyst may slip into a coercive approach.

A negotiative approach aims to bring the analyst and the group into an agreement about the problem or opportunity by the analyst first starting with an empathetic style and encouraging a lot of debate and discussion. This is followed by a period of negotiation where a clear statement is developed with which the group is prepared to agree and which summarizes the problem or opportunity to the satisfaction of the analyst. The key point is that both the analyst and the group members should feel that the statement is a satisfactory reflection of the discussion and, although there may be some disagreement about matters of detail, there should be agreement on the main points. Whatever disagreements are evident should be recorded for later study and discussion because they may indicate hitherto unexplored facets of the problem or opportunity.

Problem definition
What techniques can be used to assist people in discussing problems?

A useful technique is to develop a model or 'rich picture' which serves as a record of, and guide to, the problem; the technique is sometimes called 'mapping'. The technique has been described by Wood-Harper.[2] The aim is to produce a diagram of the problem as perceived both objectively and subjectively by those involved. The picture will identify the stakeholders, what is being done and the internal and operating environments insofar as they are considered to have any bearing on the problem. The purpose is to draw together the threads of the problem as perceived by all participants, thus providing a basis for debate and understanding of the problem; consideration of solutions is deliberately forestalled by quite detailed analysis thus preventing premature, and often mistaken, attempts at solutions.

To start making a 'rich picture', at the centre of a piece of paper draw a box and label it with the name of the organization or unit of the organization which is the centre of concern. Identify, with suitable symbols or words, the other people and activities linked with this concern. Crossed swords can be used to indicate areas where disputes or conflict can arise and boxes can be used to record the worries of the participants most concerned with the problem. It may be necessary to spread a complicated picture over several sheets, each dealing with one aspect of the organization or problem, but try to confine it to one sheet. This will have the effect of encouraging the group to justify the inclusion of each component and the process should facilitate the development of a clearer view of the problem. An illustration of the 'rich picture' approach is given in case study 1.

Case study 1: problem definition at Uplands University

Jeremy Fisher, the Librarian of Uplands University, was in a hurry. Today was not a good day on which to arrive late and he was conscious of several glances in his direction as he entered the concrete and glass building which housed the Library. Next week there was to be a meeting of the Library Committee and his mind was on the business of the meeting as he climbed the stairs to his office. Usher, the new Professor of History, intended to raise the matter of setting up a departmental library: 'A special collection linked to our new course', she had called it but Fisher recognized this seemingly innocuous suggestion as an attempt at breaching the Vice-Chancellor's policy of centralization of resources. It would swiftly become the Library of the History Department, he had no doubt, and would begin to drain resources from the University Library. Fisher had to oppose it and he needed to consider what strategy would best serve:

in particular, who could he persuade to be on his side?

Two memoranda were on his desk, together with the morning's post. He dealt with the letters swiftly and turned his attention to the first memorandum. It was from the Registrar's Department, informing him that no applications for the two posts in the Bibliographic Services section had been received. This was a major blow: Fred Cox, the Head of Section, had been complaining for weeks about the work load his staff were having to endure as a result of the resignation of two assistants some three months ago. Fred would just have to be patient a little longer, he decided, until a re-advertisement of the posts could appear. Fisher penned an commiseratory note to Cox and set the memorandum aside for further consideration. Perhaps May would be a better time to advertise, when the young hopefuls in schools of librarianship were nearing their release onto the job market.

The second memorandum was from Dr Robert Jenkins, Senior Lecturer in the Department of Physics. Fisher knew him quite well: Jenkins was a member of the Library Committee and reckoned to be influential in the politicking which made life at Uplands occasionally fascinating but always enervating. Jenkins wished to draw attention to the time it had taken for a new publication he had requested to arrive. Did Fisher think that three months was too long, taking into consideration the fact that the book had been widely advertised and freely available in the University bookshop for some six weeks? The tone of the memorandum seemed quite good humoured but Fisher decided to treat this enquiry with some caution and annotated the memorandum for the attention of Brenda Strong, Head of the Reader Services section, with a copy to Fred Cox. Now he could get on with planning his strategy for the Library Committee meeting.

The answers from Brenda Strong and Fred Cox came that afternoon. The swiftness of the responses surprised Fisher: he wondered whether he had touched upon a nerve. On reading the replies he saw that the lines for a pitched battle were being drawn. Strong confirmed the date of Jenkins' request and the date of supply of the item; moreover, she indicated in her precise and somewhat acerbic style that this was not the only example of delays in supply and that she had received many complaints over a period of some months. The problem was certainly not with her section: as soon as items were received from Bibliographic Services they were passed, within one day, on to the readers who had requested them. The reputation of her section and, by implication, the University Library and all its staff was being assailed by inefficiency in the Bibliographic Services section. Fisher groaned inwardly, recognizing that this could well turn into another of Brenda's crusades which would leave groups of staff in sullen confrontation in the staff room and staff meetings for some weeks to come.

Even Fred Cox's usual mild approach seemed to have deserted him: his reply was brief and forceful. How did Fisher think that items could be processed swiftly without staff? The cataloguing backlog alone amounted to some 12 weeks.

Fisher decided that it would be best for a group discussion of the problem to be initiated. Neither Cox nor Strong had made any suggestions in their replies for alleviating the problem and Fisher suspected that neither was ready to think rather than react. Fisher hoped that a meeting would enable both to discharge their feelings and then turn to developing a solution. Fisher, Strong and Cox usually got on together quite well, each respecting the expertise of the others.

The meeting took place the next day. Fisher asked Brenda Strong to summarize the points made in her written reply. She had calmed down somewhat and simply confirmed the details given by Jenkins in his original memorandum. She then produced a list of similar complaints from other academic staff and students which her staff had received orally during the last fortnight. Throughout this Fred Cox listened without reacting: he seemed to be biding his time. Eventually, Strong concluded her report with the phrase, 'Now it's your problem: what are you going to do about it?' This seemed to be aimed at Cox, though Fisher felt that he was also a target for blame in Strong's eyes.

Before letting Cox respond, Fisher outlined his understanding of the events and tried to summarize Strong's discontent. 'I am sure we share your concern about this problem,' he said, 'and we must work on a solution together.' Fisher emphasized the last word, trying to build up a sense of cooperation within the group. Cox nodded his agreement; Strong sighed and said, 'Yes, I suppose so.'

Now it was the turn of Fred Cox. He started calmly enough, outlining the date of the original order and the date of its receipt. He also verified the fact that it had taken four weeks for the item to be processed through his section. He explained that even this was faster than the time it took to process other materials: his section had a special 'fast service' for requested items. The main problem was staff, he said: the section was short of two assistants and had never really recovered from the restructuring of staff which had taken place one year ago. This process had reduced the number of assistants in his section by one, so he was really three short, he said. In addition, he strongly objected to the present policy whereby new staff were attached to his section for initial training and then moved on to other sections: 'We're always having to work with inexperienced staff,' he said, 'and it takes much longer to get anything done.' He had become more animated and Fisher sensed that this was a problem about which Cox had been worrying for some time.

Brenda Strong was the next to speak. Fisher could see that she had also sensed Cox's concern and was prepared to support him. As so often, Fisher thought, what had appeared to be an obvious problem, susceptible to an easy solution, had turned out to be a symptom of a deeper disease. He was tempted to propose action, to begin re-planning the staff structure and considering the implications of the training policy, but he forbore, recognizing that there was much to be gained by further discussion. Confidence of staff and good morale were also vital if the library service was to seek to repair the damage done by its deteriorating service. He suspected that questions, similar to those raised in Jenkins' original memorandum, might well be raised at the forthcoming Library Committee meeting and he wished to be able to give a realistic response.

'Let's record our concerns,' he said, and crossed to a whiteboard in his office. Cox and Strong had been present at several meetings where Fisher had used the technique of the 'rich picture' as an aid to problem definition; both had been sceptical at first but they had later admitted that it often released ideas and views that had later proved helpful in developing solutions. During the next fifteen minutes, a 'rich picture' (Figure 9) was drawn. As the diagram developed, Fisher checked that he had correctly recorded their thoughts.

'I have something else to add,' said Fisher, as the diagram was nearing completion. He outlined the suggestion about establishing a special collection, made by Usher, and his fears about the way in which such a proposal might develop into a departmental library. 'The resource implications could be serious: we might be called upon to supply two assistants, at least, to cover opening hours and tidy it up.' Cox and Strong could see that this development would precipitate a staffing crisis and were content to see it added to the 'rich picture'.

Feeling that the meeting had got as far as was then useful, Fisher summarized their findings: a shortfall of staff in one section compounded by unhelpful arrangements over staff training were leading to a deterioration in the request service sufficient for it to have been noticed by several users. The proposed development by the History Department could place an additional staffing burden on the Library.

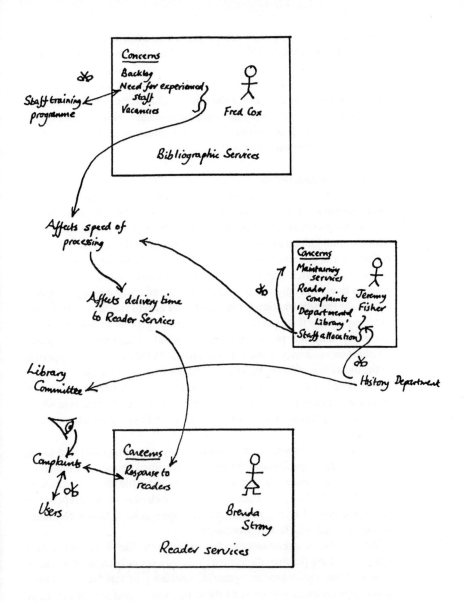

Figure 9 Rich picture

61

After the meeting, Fisher contemplated the whiteboard. He now felt more confident about the Library Committee meeting. After all, Bob Jenkins would see the point: the request service would certainly not improve if staff resources were drained off to run a special service in another department and, as for the other problem, he could already see ways in which the training plan could be amended. Now, whom did he know in a school of librarianship who could suggest some likely candidates for the vacant posts?

Exploring opportunities

It is quite difficult for people to conjure ideas out of thin air: most need some stimulus, or framework, and time before ideas will flow freely. Part of the problem is a reluctance to take the risk of revealing an idea which is then judged to be silly or unworkable by others. The risk which is taken is the potential loss or reduction of one's expert power. Power is something which depends on the perception of others: expertise, as a power base, will only last as long as other members of a group recognize a need for the information it represents and accept that it is correct. An idea, especially if it is novel, is on uncertain ground in both respects: the group may not regard it as being useful or appropriate in given circumstances or may dispute its soundness. In either case, the expertise of the individual offering the idea will be diminished in the eyes of others, hence there is a reluctance to offer ideas unless the thinker believes they will be acceptable to the group. It is this process of self-evaluation which serves to throttle the creation of novel ideas and radical departures from the norm.

In some circumstances, this restraint may be appropriate and to the benefit of the organization: given a well-defined problem, little room for manoeuvre over the use of resources and little time in which to produce a solution, few managers would welcome or be prepared to accept the risk of trying an entirely new approach. A 'quick fix' tends to follow tried and tested procedures.

More extensive alterations may be needed in the life of an organization when something perturbs the system. This may occur because of a change in any of the environments, general, operating or internal. A change in the general environment is likely to be gradual and will affect many other systems and organizations in society. There will be time to consider, analyse and prepare a strategy; in addition, since other organizations will be affected, there will be an opportunity to consult and to plan in consort. The effects of change at this level will be long term and will fundamentally affect the society and culture in which they occur. Changes in technology, political climate, the economy and the law constitute examples of this kind of change.

Changes in the operating and internal environments are likely to be perceived more directly and will have a more immediate effect. In addition, because of this immediacy, it may appear that the effect is more marked, more focussed, perhaps targeted on part of a system though the effect will eventually be apparent in all parts.

It is possible that the management may feel the need for change: the organization may be thought to need expansion, contraction, or a shift in its objectives. In essence, this is no different than a change in the internal environment: the management are reacting to something perceived in the general or operating environments. For example, the senior management of a commercial organization may decide to expand the company by acquisition: the pressure to which the senior management is responding may be from shareholders or competitors forming some of the 'stakeholder' groups in the operating environment. The acquisition will change the internal environment of the company as the personnel, practices and objectives of the acquired company are absorbed. This will have an effect on, for example, a company information service which will need to respond to this alteration in the internal environment of the company. Similarly, the staff of the acquired company will need to respond to changes in their internal environment.

Although change brings with it sets of problems, it also presents opportunities: a time, a juncture or a combination of things which are favourable to some end or purpose. A task of management is to seek out such opportunities by regularly scanning the environments for evidence of a developing pressure for change.

The goals, or missions, of an organization are essentially long term: they represent the 'big' statements about its intended influence in society. Generally, these remain unchanged throughout the life of an organization; it is the objectives, which point to ways in which the goals can be attained, that change with the emergence of opportunities. Thus, a college library may have a goal of supporting the research work of the institution, this to be achieved through the objective of providing fast access to relevant subject collections for all staff conducting research. The development of online information retrieval services has provided an opportunity to step nearer the goal by providing access to relevant databases of information to complement subject collections. Thus the objective has been changed as a result of both a long-term change in the general environment – the development of computer and telecommunications technology – and a change in the operating environment – the establishment of firms providing databases and firms offering access to such resources. Before such developments can be incorporated within the range of activities considered acceptable by the management of the library it is necessary for the developments to be recognized as opportunities which are coherent and in accord with the its goals.

Having accepted that it is necessary for an organization which wishes to remain successful to take advantage of whatever opportunities are recognized to be feasible and appropriate, it is time to return to the problems of exploring such opportunities.

It is necessary to foster the development of conditions in which evaluation is suppressed, at least at the outset, when ideas are being generated. To this end, the technique known as 'brainstorming' is often recommended. There are several ways in which sessions using this technique can be run but the critical point is that participants should be prepared and set at ease. The guidance given in chapter 2 about the functions of the systems analyst indicates ways in which members of a group can be helped to relax and to share their ideas. It is most important that the analyst, or group leader, should explain the 'rules', emphasizing that evaluative remarks of approval or disapproval should be reserved for later. The emphasis should be on developing as many ideas as possible, thus providing a large bank which can then be screened for feasibility and acceptability. Participants should be encouraged to exchange 'wild' ideas, too – suppressing ideas through critical self-evaluation can lead to some interesting opportunities being neglected. What may appear wild and impracticable to one may be feasible in another's view and may start a train of thought which can lead to other exciting ideas. It is helpful to start a brainstorming session with a broad statement of need to give the imagination of each participant a free rein, later allowing the group to focus upon particulars. A session might be started with a statement such as, 'What does "user satisfaction" mean?' and then lead on to considering the opportunities for achieving greater user satisfaction afforded by the development of a new current-awareness service.

Some means of recording ideas is needed. It is sometimes suggested that a tape-recorder should be used: the argument is that participants quickly lose whatever 'microphone shyness' they may have and the tape then preserves every nuance of the discussion: nothing is lost. In practice, there are several problems. Firstly, to make sure the remarks of every participant are recorded intelligibly requires the use of several microphones; ideally, each participant should wear a microphone so that comments can be recorded whatever the physical position of the participant. Few people can really relax in such circumstances unless they have some experience of being recorded in this way. Secondly, the use of several microphones will necessitate using a mixing desk and the balancing of inputs from the microphones to ensure that each participant is audible. Thirdly, the transcription of the tape is necessary if an easily assimilated record is to be produced for detailed study: this is a difficult task, even for an experienced audio-typist, because several people may be talking at once and the flow of ideas in the written record may then seem confused. This is one area where technology may impede rather than facilitate progress.

The use of flip-charts provides a cheap format which is visible by everyone in the group and a form which is semi-permanent. A problem with their use is that whoever is designated as recorder may be inhibited by having to spend time in writing the group comments and will be left out of the group exchange. This difficulty may be overcome if the analyst is able to take on this role which is, in any case, consonant with the duties of a group facilitator. The drawing of a 'rich picture' of the current state of the organization may be helpful, especially if every member can be encouraged to participate. The view offered by the rich picture may also suggest other avenues for exploration.

Kotler[3] suggests three ways in which creativity may be stimulated. The first, attribute listing, consists of analysing an activity, service or idea and then considering how it can be changed to increase its potential to give satisfaction. Thus, the reference enquiry process might be broken down into several steps: query statement, query negotiation, translation into terms appropriate for the information retrieval system, determination of strategy, and so on. Then, considering each step, alternative ways of doing the job could be discussed. The step of query negotiation, for example, might be aided by the use of an 'expert system' to explore the nature and depth of the enquiry and to suggest alternative ways of specifying the problem.

The second procedure for stimulating creativity is that of forcing relationships: list several system components and then consider each in relation to the others. An example might be reference collections, telecommunication networks and databases, where an analysis of possible relationships could suggest that reference resources be concentrated at one service point, others being linked to it by a digital telecommunications network allowing access to a database of answers to the most frequent enquiries.

Problem analysis, the third procedure, reinforces the notion that a problem and an opportunity are complementary. In this procedure, the users of a service are asked for a list of the problems and frustrations they encounter. Each problem or frustration can be the source of an opportunity to develop and improve the service. Users of an academic library might suggest, for example, that it is sometimes difficult to go to the library to reserve items. The library managers might think of allowing users to make reservations through the campus telecommunications network which would also be available out of library opening hours, thus taking the opportunity of expanding access.

Creative thinking can be encouraged by two other techniques. The first is called 'position analysis', sometimes called 'SWOT analysis', this name being derived from the initial letters of the four characteristics of an organization which enter into the analysis, namely, *strengths*, *weaknesses*, *opportunities* and *threats* (see Figure 10). The technique is useful as means of opening discussion and as a means of structuring debate.

The analysis of strengths, weaknesses, opportunities and threats offers a quick means of establishing the position of the organization with respect to present and future lines of endeavour. The analysis can be conducted as an informal, participative, 'brainstorming' session or could form the basis of a regular, formal, assessment conducted by one or several managers. The factors operating in each of the quadrants can be expressed in whatever way is considered helpful for the problem in hand: sometimes a brief 'qualitative' statement may be sufficient, but a detailed 'quantitative' statement may sometimes be needed.

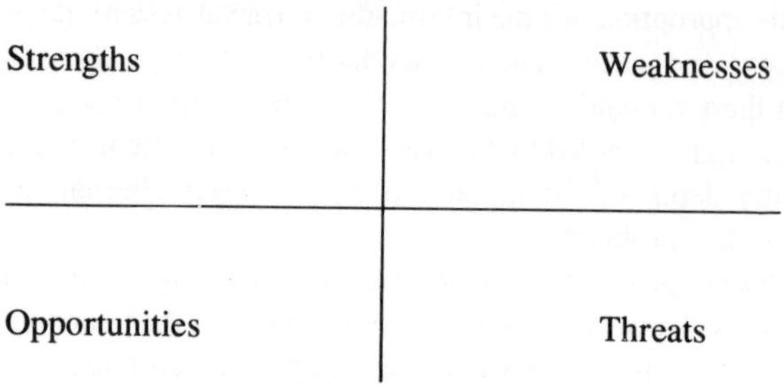

Strengths	Weaknesses
Opportunities	Threats

Figure 10   Position analysis

Strengths and *weaknesses* refer, within the context of a position analysis, to factors in the organization occurring in the internal and operating environments and, therefore, capable of being controlled or influenced by the organization. A low turnover of professional staff or an efficient cataloguing process could be regarded as strengths whilst lengthy waiting times for reserved items or declining numbers of registered users could represent weaknesses. Identifying a weakness is a useful step towards improvement because it suggests the need for the investment of resources to redress it. However important this may be, there may be an understandable reluctance by group members to identify weaknesses, especially if such identification would imply an indirect criticism of another manager. This underlines the need to conduct this aspect of the analysis carefully and in a non-evaluative manner. The analyst should beware, however, of allowing a group to dwell too long on one aspect: it is easy, for example, to build up good feeling by listing many strengths and few weaknesses. A balance between the two is unlikely to occur, but a sustained effort should be made to develop both lists. In addition, it is useful to ask a contributor to state briefly why an aspect is considered to be a strength or weakness. The analyst should be careful not to encourage evaluation of such statements: it is better to leave this until a later stage.

Opportunities and *threats* refer to factors present in the operating and general environments over which the organization may not necessarily have any means of direct control or influence. Changes in the general environment, such as those in the political life of a country and developments in technology, may pose threats and opportunities, as may changes in the operating environment such as the emergence of groups of potential users or the development of competition. These factors may be complementary: for example, does the development of fact retrieval databases pose a competitive threat to existing reference library services, especially if they can be used quite easily by unskilled searchers, or can it provide an opportunity for the existing reference service to offer training and advice as an extension of its other activities? The position analysis can provide a useful focus for the discussion of management attitudes to such developments. It is important, however, to guard against the view that every threat can be turned into an opportunity: some threats, especially those in the general environment, are not susceptible to being transmuted in this way because they affect fundamental principles on which the service offered by the organization is based. For example, the move towards direct charging for services threatens the concept of a 'free' public library service, as presently understood in the United Kingdom. There is no sense in which the development could be regarded as an opportunity because any opportunities that might be recognized would arise from a service based upon the fundamentally different premise of direct charging. This also underlines the point that the detection and analysis of threats is vital to the continuing existence of an organization; without such review the management of an organization would be unable to signal the need for a redefinition of its goals and principles of operation.

Some threats can be countered; a strategy can be developed which will minimize their effects. Usually, such threats arise in the operating environment and pose a challenge to objectives rather than goals. For example, a price increase for the use of certain frequently used databases might pose a threat to the financial viability of a commercial information department. Possible strategies would be to seek to use them through another online host; to use other databases having similar subject coverage; to switch to manual searching or to purchase copies of the databases for in-house use. The choice of strategy will depend on comparing the level of service which each of these approaches could offer. An objective of seeking to minimize expenditure would remain unchanged by such strategies only if the approach with the lowest cost also offers a similar, or better, level of service to that of the original.

The purpose of the position analysis is to enable the management of an organization to determine its present position in relation to the environments and to begin to define the gap between this position and where it would like to be. The opportunities suggest paths towards such aspirations.

Many opportunities for service organizations are concerned with developing the range of services, improving some component of a service or supplying services to a a group other than those already served: the opportunities are about products and markets. This is unsurprising because the pressure for change from the general and operating environments is likely to emanate principally from two sources: users and those who are funding the service, either directly through fees or indirectly through community service charges. The pressures will be for the supply of additional, or different, services to existing groups of users and, from the funders, for charges to be minimized. In many cases, the funders and the users comprise the same group but represent different 'stakeholder' views, the users being interested in service effectiveness, the funders with its efficiency. A healthy tension results from this combination of pressures because it is apparent to the manager that an organization must respond to the changing and increasing needs of users by developing strategies which also take into account costs and effects of change on existing services.

The response of the management of an organization can take several forms. Aspiring to greater effectiveness may mean developing a strategy which tries to complement services already provided to existing groups but it may also mean extending services to other groups. A strategy for improving efficiency may include devising improved methods for its delivery but it may also mean trying to reduce its unit cost by increasing the pool of users.

The second method of stimulating ideas is useful in encouraging managers to consider the strategies by which opportunities outlined above may be realized. A strategy is a statement about how a particular objective is to be attained: in many circumstances more than one strategy may be possible. Some means of selecting the best strategy in particular circumstances must be used.

The product/market matrix devised by H. Igor Ansoff[4] serves as a useful tool for examining strategies; Figure 11 shows the matrix.

P R O D U C T S

		Existing	New
M			
A R	Existing	Market penetration	Product extension
K			
E			
T S	New	Market extension	Diversification

Figure 11, part 1   Product/market matrix

69

- *Markets* may be identifiable groups of existing or new users, or groups of non-users
- *Products* may be tangible items (e.g. bibliographies, documents) or intangibles like services (e.g. question-answering, end-user search training)
- *Market penetration*: growth is sought through taking existing products into new markets
- *Product extension*: growth is sought through developing improved and new products for existing markets
- *Diversification*: growth is sought by entering new markets with new products. This strategy is 'high risk' because there will be a lack of experience with both the product and the market

Figure 11, part 2

This diagram tries to focus attention on the marketing strategies open to enterprises. In essence, for library and information services, the markets are represented by different market segments, each segment being a group of users or potential users which can be identified as sharing similar needs and with which a channel of communication can be opened. The 'opportunities' section of the SWOT analysis represents groups which are distinguishable and reachable, whilst the Ansoff matrix allows the manager to consider the marketing strategy to reach such groups and the risk associated with such strategies. Diversification, represented in the Ansoff matrix by providing new products in new markets, is a very high-risk strategy because of lack of knowledge of the user group and the product. To be successful, considerable resources must be allocated to exploring the market and testing products. This is a strategy which is associated with the exploratory forecasting dimension of planning described in chapter 1. Market penetration, on the other hand, is represented in the Ansoff matrix by increasing the level of demand in existing markets for existing products. It is a low-risk strategy, which might derive from normative forecasting and would offer a path to achieving the objective of greater efficiency. Product development and market extension offer medium-level risks and represent the interaction between exploratory and normative forecasting.

Some strategies will, therefore, be viewed as being more attractive because they offer lower risks. Another way of looking at this choice is to consider the investment of resources necessary, not only in terms of equipment and facilities but also in terms of learning about the product and the needs of users. Here again, it is evident that a strategy which uses an existing product or an existing market will prove more attractive provided the accrued benefits to the organization are considered to be great enough.

Case study 2: opportunities at Uplands University

The meeting of the Library Committee had gone quite well: all the business had been completed and the Librarian, Jeremy Fisher, was confident that the Policy and Resources Committee would agree to the various proposals that had been presented. The problem over delays in supplying requested items (see case study 1) had been raised, as he had suspected might happen, but armed with some ideas developed during his meeting with Brenda Strong, Head of the Reader Services section, and Fred Cox, Head of the Bibliographic Services section, he had been able to reassure the Committee that matters were under control and significant improvements should shortly prove possible. He had shared with them his concern about lack of staff in the Bibliographic Services section and mentioned that another review of the disposition of staff resources would be necessary in the near future. There had been some discussion of this, with everyone commenting on the adverse effect that low salaries in the university sector were having on attracting good applicants for any kind of job.

Fisher had arranged for the next item on the agenda to be a request from Professor Usher for the establishment of a special collection to be housed in the Department of History; the collection was linked to the development of a new course to be run next academic year by the Department. It would need some materials to be transferred from the Library and a member of staff to administer and tidy it from time to time; the bulk of the collection would be provided by the Department, however. In thinking about the proposal before the meeting of the Library Committee took place, Fisher had developed a suspicion that the special collection might swiftly become the Library of the History Department and would begin to drain resources from the University Library. He had decided to oppose the idea because resources, especially staff, were already in short supply. It would make more sense for the Department to donate the embryo collection to the Library, he thought.

He had expected some support for his opposition from other members of the Library Committee and had, indeed, indulged in some discreet lobbying to ensure that members were aware of his fears. Much to his dismay he found that several were in favour of the suggestion provided it did not affect the services in the University Library; 'asking for the moon' was how Fisher described this expectation to his senior staff the next day. He had argued against the idea for some time in the Library Committee meeting but with little success: the Committee had asked him to consider the idea more fully and to report to its next meeting. Fisher strongly suspected that ulterior motives were present: several members could see some advantage for their own departments if an attempt at breaching the Vice-Chancellor's policy of centralization of resources should prove successful. The principle would have been lost and other 'specialized' facilities might soon be expected to appear.

'I don't think the VC will allow this to go through,' he said, in the senior staff meeting next day, 'but we're committed to studying the suggestion, even if we believe it will be a waste of time. So, how shall we proceed?' Including himself, there were seven present at the staff meeting and, as they represented all sectors of the work of the University Library, he thought it would prove a good forum for a discussion.

Fairly quickly, the group decided that it would be best to deal with Usher's proposal on its stated terms. It should be seen as a request to meet a particular need of the Department of History: the political implications should be set aside because they were primarily the concern of the Vice-Chancellor and the Policy and Resources Committee. In addition, it was agreed that Professor Usher should be invited along to discuss the needs of the Department. This would enable everyone in the group to have first-hand knowledge of the proposal and an opportunity to discuss any problems with existing services which might emerge.

The meeting took place three days later. Professor Usher was pleased to be invited and she commented favourably on the readiness of the staff to respond to her suggestion, quite unlike, she said, other library services she could name! Fisher was polite, but non-committal, in his reply: he wished the meeting to consider the proposal dispassionately and he thought the compliments might be a ploy to 'soften-up' any opposition.

Usher then outlined her proposal: the new course was concerned with the history of the newspaper industry from early broadsheets through to the present day. She had brought along some of the materials which would form part of the special collection: there were facsimiles of early newspapers, documents, slides and other material. In addition, there was an extensive book list. Some 20 students were enrolled and the course was expected to grow in popularity. The proposal to the Library Committee had arisen because of a decision about the teaching method: students were each to be assigned to a work group; each group would study a range of materials dealing with a particular theme in some detail and then report to a weekly plenary session. The topics had been chosen to be sufficiently distinct to avoid one group needing access to material being studied by another group in the same week. The problem was the loan policy of the University Library: material in demand was restricted to a short loan collection which allowed loans of two items only for three hours at a time. What the students of the Department would need would be access to up to 15 items for two or three days at a time. The 'special collection' was the only way the Department believed students could have satisfactory access.

There was a long silence when she had finished. Fisher invited comment but it was clear, from the few responses, that time for digestion of the idea was needed. He decided that it would be helpful to consider the position of the Library in relation to the idea. Accordingly, he suggested that the group use the 'SWOT' technique, a method that the group had used on previous occasions.

The strengths were quickly identified: the collections already included a lot of material relating to the social and legal aspects of the press, especially from the mid-nineteenth century on. This material had been donated to the Library some years ago and, despite being a fine collection, had not attracted much use. Usher, previously unaware of the existence of the collection, was very interested. Another strength was that David Smith, a member of the staff of the Library who had a particular interest in the subject, had assumed some responsibility for maintaining and adding to the collection. Fisher was pleased that this had been raised because he had been concerned, for some time, that resources were being devoted to building up a collection for which there appeared to be little need. He had been meaning to discuss this with Smith but had delayed because of his reluctance to interfere with an aspect of professional work in which a colleague obviously found job satisfaction.

The weaknesses were considered to be the loan policy and the lack of staff to administer a special collection. At this point, Professor Usher intervened. Surely, she said, these weaknesses were mutually exclusive: if the Library was responsible for supplying materials to the students then the loan policy would be a weakness but the policy would not be significant if the Department housed the collection. In the latter case, however, lack of staff to administer it would become a problem. Fisher agreed but explained that in trying to assess a position it was helpful to bring out all the significant points without making prior judgement about the strategy to be followed. In any case, he suggested, the availability of library staff would be a limiting factor on the pursuance of any strategy until such time as some of the vacant positions had been filled and the use of staff resources had been reassessed.

Several members considered that possible loss of control over library resources would pose a threat. It would be sensible to transfer some materials from the University Library to the special collection of the Department, if it came into being, but this would remove such material from easy use by students and staff in other departments. Fisher was not convinced that this was likely to pose much of a threat because little interest had, up to this point, been shown in the material already held in the Library collection. He reserved his comment for later, however, not wishing to interrupt the flow of discussion.

It was when they came to consider opportunities that the discussion flagged. Apart from a suggestion that it would be a good opportunity for the Library to become more involved in the process of course design, nobody had much to contribute. Fisher decided to try another approach to see if this would encourage the group. He thought the technique of 'forced relationships' would be useful so he suggested that the group members should list the significant resources in the sections of the Library for which each was responsible and then consider each in relation to the needs identified by Professor Usher. Nothing much came of this until Brenda Strong mentioned the library seminar room which was, she said, greatly under-used. Apart from some library instruction seminars held at the start of the academic year and the occasional meeting it had no regular use. Usher showed some interest in this, explaining that an unresolved problem for the History Department was to find a room in which the 'special collection' could be housed and to which students could have access at all reasonable hours. Would the Library consider housing the collection in the library seminar room? Fisher allowed discussion of the pros and cons of the idea to continue for some time: it was evident that there was no sustained opposition to the idea. He suggested that it would have to be clearly understood that the room would remain under the control of the Library and that other meetings could be held there, when necessary; he agreed that it would be fairly easy to arrange matters to avoid conflict over use. Strong suggested that the donated collection be moved to the library seminar room; Usher agreed that this would be useful and asked whether David Smith could continue his work in maintaining the collection and extend his interest to the special collection from the History Department.

'What about loans?' enquired Fred Cox, 'Isn't that still going to be a problem?' It was Usher who replied. The Library would be open for far longer hours than any rooms in the History Department, she explained; if the access was better, there would be less need for students to borrow materials. Brenda Strong suggested that it would, in any case, be fairly easy to arrange for a longer loan period for items from the donated and special collections in case of special needs: she thought the circulation control system could be configured to accept an extra loan period category.

Fisher was pleased that an opportunity had now been clearly identified: the donated collection and the library seminar room, both hitherto under-used resources, would help to link the use of the Library with course development. A working relationship of this kind would be useful politically, too. Also, there would now be a stronger sanction for the work of collection development which Smith had been undertaking and a more coherent base from which to argue the case for increased resources.

The meeting concluded with Fisher asking Strong to write a short report for circulation amongst the participants, further consideration of which would then form the basis for his report to the Library Committee. He felt that a significant step had been taken, the Library would remain in control of its resources and he was confident that the threat to the centralization policy had been dealt with quite effectively. He had been persuaded to concede the case for Smith extending his work of collection management but he judged the benefits of the opportunity to be great enough to outweigh the diversion of a little more of Smith's professional time. It would be good for Smith, in any case, to have more professional responsibility passed his way. The administration of the collection, its presentation, arrangement and tidying, would be an additional burden on staff but he felt confident that it could be accommodated within the review of the use of staff resources that he was now planning to initiate.

As the meeting broke up, Usher commented on how impressed she had been by the use of the 'SWOT' analysis: 'I'll have to try it in our Departmental meetings,' she joked, as they parted.

Cost – benefit analysis

The main question confronting the manager thinking about launching a project is whether the returns will be great enough to justify the initial outlay and running costs. Cost – benefit analysis is a technique which is often recommended for guiding judgements of this kind. In the commercial sector of the operating environment, where a project concerns a product or service which is to be sold, there is a tangible return in the form of profits or losses. In a 'not-for-profit' sector the return is less apparent and, hence, more difficult to quantify. Cost–benefit analysis is too useful a technique to be neglected despite this difficulty, however.

The source of the difficulty is a lack of agreement on how benefits should be represented in monetary terms. Money is used because it is a medium in which both sides of the project equation can be represented in common units and compared. Express costs in money terms and compare their total with the total of benefits, also expressed in money terms: this is the essence of cost–benefit analysis. A little thought may lead one to suspect that commercial organizations also recognize returns other than direct profits and losses. It is often argued that a commercial organization exists only to make money and will assess any opportunity solely in these terms. This view may be true in some sectors, but many organizations also give money to charities, become patrons of the arts, sponsor professorial chairs in academic institutions and assist with the cost of training individuals. The immediate benefits to the organization are publicity, visibility of the company and its products, and the creation and maintenance of a certain image, considered desirable. In the longer term, the company *may* benefit through increased sales but it is doubtful whether anyone could demonstrate a strong link between the investment and the return. Thus, in some respects, the profit-making and the 'not-for-profit' sectors are comparable: managers in both sectors must be prepared to recognize and judge the value of some returns in terms other than money.

Wherever possible it is of immediate help to management for returns to be translated into money. This will involve some agreement on a method by which monetary value may be ascribed to a return. In libraries and information services, where selling information or access to information is, at present, still rare, the benefits may be expressed as time saving and saving on other resources, together with external benefits. Externalities, as they are sometimes called, represent benefits or costs to third parties as a result of the use of a product or service. For example, members of a family may benefit as a result of a holiday planned after one of them has read a travel guide; alternatively, the members might suffer because of a lack of good reference books outlining the advantages and disadvantages of particular careers.

A consideration of externalities is of clear importance in considering projects in libraries and information services. Many of the benefits, and some of the costs, will fall into the category of externalities: the benefit of recreational reading, for example, is evident in the lives of many individuals but it also has an effect on those within their social groups and on the nature of society as a whole. Any attempt at precise quantification will be unsuccessful because the benefits are unpredictable, confounded with benefits accruing from other sources, such as film or television viewing, and only perceptible over a long period of time. Many would argue that activities which lead to such benefits fall into the category of 'public good' − something which is undertaken and paid for by a society because it represents part of a civilized culture. It might also be argued that recognizing the value of such benefits and being prepared to manage an enterprise to enhance the benefits to society is what marks out the area of professional expertise. Professionally qualified librarians and information workers are, on the basis of this argument, the people best able to think about the effects that access to documents and information will have on society and to make choices on behalf of the society.

Hamburg[5] has proposed an elaborate planning system in which benefits are measured in terms of increased 'document exposure'. His proposition is that the goal of any library or information service is to ensure that its clients have access to appropriate documents, or the information they contain, at the time when it is needed. All activities, projects and services are assessed in terms of the effect they will have on the measure of document exposure. The use of so-called 'proxy measures' of this kind can make the task of project evaluation easier though the argument about the extent of the effect, and thus the value to be assigned, will still be necessary and the process of computing measures may be rather tedious. The end result will be a statement showing that, for a particular project, a certain expenditure will lead to an increase or decrease in document exposure.

Estimates of costs will need to be included in a feasibility study (see the following section) and will form part of the cost−benefit analysis. At this stage only estimates of outline costs will normally be available because no detailed plans will have been drawn up. An exception may be where the project is restricted to the purchase and installation of equipment or service at a fixed cost or where recent previous experience of similar equipment and services can render very reliable estimates. In all other cases, some allowance should be made for unexpected additional costs.

In determining costs it is important to determine the *economic costs* of a project. It is tempting simply to list items of expenditure covering both capital outlay and, if appropriate, running costs over several years. The economic cost will include such outlays but will also include the *opportunity costs* of all resources used in the project.

An opportunity cost is incurred whenever resources which are in limited supply are devoted to one use rather than another: the cost is represented by the value which could have accrued from the rejected use. The value that could be used by the next best use of the resources represents the opportunity cost. To take a simple example, suppose a limited amount of money is available to fund either the purchase of 200 books or ten journal subscriptions. The opportunity cost of buying the books is represented by the benefits which might have accrued from the 10 journal subscriptions foregone and vice versa if the subscriptions are purchased instead of the books. In some cases, the benefit can be expressed in money terms. For example, a commercial organization would view the opportunity cost of its information service as the income that might have accrued if the money invested in establishing and running the service had, instead, been invested on the money market. The opportunity cost of using a photocopier to produce the internal company information bulletin is the profit which might have been made by using it to produce something which might be sold at a profit. Not every item merits consideration of this kind: the opportunity cost associated with using a specialized machine which cannot be used for any other purpose is nil because no alternative use has been forgone; its *purchase* would, however, incur an opportunity cost because the capital outlay could have been used for investment or for other projects with associated benefits.

When comparing project costs it is important to ensure that the costs have been calculated using the same assumptions and cost structures. Check, for example, whether overhead costs have been included and whether they are charged as a fixed proportion or whether they vary with levels of production. The key point is to make sure that the estimates of project costs can be truly compared.

Cost–benefit analysis should be based on economic costs. To illustrate this, consider the project outlined in case study 2. The capital outlay might include extra shelving and signs; direct running costs might include stationery, new materials added to the collection and some maintenance and staff time; indirect costs might include a proportion of heating, lighting and building maintenance costs. The opportunity costs to the university will include interest forgone on the capital outlay and interest forgone over time on the money spent on running costs. The Librarian might also wish to consider the value which might be obtained if the staff time, which from the details of the case can be seen to be in short supply, was used for other important activities.

A detailed study of cost–benefit analysis techniques in relation to public sector activities is given by Henry and Haynes.[6]

In summary, cost–benefit analysis can provide some useful guidance to managers but it cannot be regarded as a substitute for either thought or the exercise of professional responsibility.

The feasibility study

New ideas are essential to development: these should be screened initially to decide whether they are acceptable and worth the further effort of a feasibility study. The function of a feasibility study is to draw attention to ill-conceived projects early enough for them to be adjusted or stopped.

Screening of new ideas should be linked back to the consideration of goals, objectives and present strategies of the organization. In particular, it is useful to reflect on whether the idea makes use of a strength or avoids dependence on some weakness of the organization. Additionally, does an idea fit in with other projects and the existing work of the organization? Is it consistent with general policy guidelines? Whilst adherence to these guidelines is not essential – there may well be fruitful ideas which lie outside the existing business of an organization – the further an idea departs from them, the greater will be the risk associated with its development. The guidelines act as criteria for filtering new ideas. If several ideas are being considered it is useful to assign weights to them relative to their satisfaction of the criteria; the ideas can then be ranked. In this way, the idea which most completely matches the criteria will appear at the top of the rank.

It is often said that any project is feasible – given infinite resources and unlimited time! The problem for all managers is deciding whether it is *beneficial* to pursue an opportunity or solve a particular problem. Commitment to an idea is a quality worth encouraging but it is also, like many powerful emotions, a potential danger. Once a project is under way, managers and staff working on its development, will have an implicit commitment to its continuance. The inertia present in any medium-size to large organization, the political relationships with stakeholders in the operating environment and the power relationships present in the internal environment make it quite difficult to stop a project once it has been launched. Even if it can be demonstrated that user needs have changed, that pressures from the environments have altered or that

79

there is now a better use for the resources being devoted to the project, the decision to wind the project up before completion will attract criticism and the suggestion that the management 'has got it wrong'.

Little wonder, then, that the first stage in the system life cycle is concerned with the assessment of feasibility. As mentioned in chapter 1, the stage of feasibility study includes problem recognition and, by extension, opportunity recognition, followed by a technical survey and economic justification. The aim is to reveal what the organization *could* be doing and allow a decision to be made on what it *should* be doing and the system or subsystem which would appear to be principally involved. Whilst it cannot warn about the kind of environmental changes, such as those outlined in the preceding paragraph, which might affect the viability of a project which is already being carried out, it can serve to warn management about projects which cannot be considered beneficial at the outset.

Because the study is driven primarily by a consideration of problems and opportunities in relation to the goals and objectives of the organization at a general level, with little attention being paid to the details of processes that may be changed, the study of this stage is sometimes referred to as a 'top-down' study.

The feasibility study is concerned with helping the manager to decide whether to commit further resources to solving a problem or responding to an opportunity. A definite decision is needed: there will be some problems which it is not worth solving − perhaps because they are trivial − or for which the solution is beyond the present resources of the general and operating environments. For example, solving the problem of the 'information rich/information poor' division in the world economy is clearly desirable and important but no solution seems affordable or technically possible at the moment. This is, of course, no argument for setting aside any further consideration of such issues; rather, it serves to highlight topics which need consideration in association with other systems in the general and operating environments. For managers to judge a solution to be feasible it is necessary for them to be confident that the necessary resources are within the control of their organization or can be obtained. For many of the major problems of society this will not be the case and it will be difficult for any organization acting on its own to declare that solutions are feasible or even possible. It is important that studies of feasibility should be realistic about the levels of resources needed and the degree of innovation that will be required.

As indicated in the discussion of problem and opportunity recognition, several strategies may be possible and another function of the feasibility study is to explore each. Some means of choosing between strategies is needed and this is usually represented in the form of filtering criteria. What criteria are used will depend on the project and the perceived needs of the organization and users, but a selection from the following list should cover most choices:

(a) degree to which the needs of users are met;
(b) benefits to users;
(c) total economic cost for implementation;
(d) running and maintenance costs;
(e) savings, both tangible and intangible;
(f) effects on the internal environment – staff, processes etc.;
(g) effects on the operating environment;
(h) time needed to develop and implement;
(i) level of risk or uncertainty associated with the development.

It is often helpful to allocate weights to these criteria, reflecting how important a particular criterion is perceived to be. The choice of weighting often reflects a resource constraint or expresses some expectation about the operating and internal environments. For example, if staff resources are known to be over-stretched, then greater attention may be focused on how a project might affect the use of those resources. This criterion might then be weighted more heavily than others. To take another example, suppose a project is to be carried out in the context of some crisis in the organization: the consequences of failure may be very severe, especially at the level of internal politics. Thus, the level of risk, as a criterion, would be weighted heavily.

The feasibility study should clarify the problem or opportunity, consider what needs to be done and arrive at a costing and a statement of benefit.

Four primary areas of feasibility are involved:

1 *Economic* feasibility – a consideration of projected development cost, compared with the income or benefit expected to be derived. A cost–benefit study, consideration of potential market growth and impact of the new 'product' on existing products, services and markets may be necessary. Economies of scale may also be defined, especially if the project will utilise existing products or existing markets.

2 *Technical* feasibility – a study of the functional and performance constraints which might affect the acceptability of the 'product'. This is often difficult to assess early in the life of a project: there is a strong

81

temptation to be optimistic. Consideration should be given to *development risk* (how great an advance beyond our known capabilities are we making?), *resource availability* (does the organization have sufficient people with the necessary skills or the potential to acquire them, access to sufficient equipment, and sufficient time?), *technology* (to what extent does the relevant technology exist?). An additional aspect which may enhance feasibility is the synergy that may arise from a small group working on a project: each may stimulate the others to produce better work.

3 *Legal and social* feasibility − a consideration of any infringements or improvements (e.g. health and safety, copyright, employment practices) which might arise from project development. Professional recognition of the worth of a project may be important here, also.

4 *Alternatives* − an evaluation of alternative approaches for project development.

The quantities of resources devoted to a feasibility study depend on the nature of the project and the attitude of the organization to risk. If the technical risk is low (for example, by using proven technology), the costs are low, the savings are large and obvious or the benefits are great, if the legal problems are insignificant and no reasonable alternative is known to exist, then there is little point in conducting a full-scale feasibility study. For example, the librarian thinking of purchasing a wordprocessing program for a microcomputer would be dealing with a known technology (provided, that is, the chosen program has been on the market for some time) available at low cost. The choice would be guided by a comparison of the wordprocessing features required with those available in the programs available, cost and availability. In many circumstances, however, the manager is unlikely to be able to be this sure. It must be understood that conducting a feasibility study, however extensive, will not make the success of the project assured. A properly conducted feasibility study will reduce uncertainty about the likely outcome and thus reduce risk but it cannot eliminate it completely.

The detailed knowledge that will be required of aims and objectives of the organization, resources available and other major factors make it desirable that the feasibility study be conducted by the systems analyst or a manager sufficiently senior to have ready access to this type of information.

The study will be submitted to the senior management for a clear decision: go ahead or stop. Only rarely should further study of feasibility be called for.

The feasibility study report

The detail and arrangement of the report may vary, but suggested headings are:

- Introduction – brief statement of problem or opportunity, significant characteristics of the environments and constraints
- Summary and recommendations
- Criteria for selection of problem solution or method of utilizing opportunity; for example, lowest cost, greatest increase in efficiency, least need for additional staff
- Alternatives – outline of possible approaches and assessment against criteria
- Fuller description of chosen approach
- Economic justification, which will include an outline of costs
- Evaluation of technical risk
- Evaluation of legal and social risks
- Congruence with existing or projected work of the organization
- Any other project-related topics

The report should be submitted to senior management and a group view formed. A clear decision needs to be taken because the next stages in the project will require the investment of more resources to promote analysis, design and implementation of the project. The delivery of the feasibility report marks the point at which development can be halted having incurred relatively little expenditure.

Notes

1   Eden, C. Jones, S. and Sims, D., *Messing about in problems: an informal structured approach to their identification and management*, Oxford, Pergamon, 1983, 18-20.

2   Wood-Harper, A. T. Antill, L. and Avison, D. E., *Information systems definition: the Multiview approach*, Oxford, Blackwell Scientific, 1985, 34-5.

3   Kotler, P. and Andreasen, A. R., *Strategic marketing for nonprofit organizations*, 3rd ed., Englewood Cliffs, New Jersey, Prentice-Hall, 1987, 384-5.

4   Ansoff, H. I., 'Strategies for diversification', *Harvard business review*, **35**, (5), 1957, 113-27.

5   Hamburg, M. *et al.*, *Library planning and decision-making systems*, Cambridge, Massachusetts, MIT, 1974, 9-39.

6   Henry, W. R. and Haynes, W. W., *Managerial economics: analysis and cases*, 4th ed., Dallas, Business Publications, 1978, 639-70.

4 *Systems analysis*

Introduction

Having reviewed the findings of the feasibility study and decided if they are favourable, the next stage in the system life cycle is *analysis*. This stage is concerned with the study of the problems of any existing system and the determination of the detailed requirements for the design of a new system. A limited range of alternatives, undiscovered during the feasibility study, may become apparent and the systems analysis will include their investigation.

From now on the commitment of resources will be greater as time, staff and materials are devoted to the project. This is a good point, therefore, to review the terms of reference of the systems analyst. The scale and extent of the project, as originally conceived, may be quite different; extra, or different, resource arrangements may now be appropriate; desirable dates for completion of the project may be different; constraints may have altered. Senior management and the analyst should discuss matters and make any adjustments that seem necessary. It is best not to leave this to chance or to assume that good relations which have been built up will necessarily be sustained without discussion and formal agreement.

The analyst has available a range of tools for the investigation. These include means of discovering facts about a system and means of describing or representing the system. There is no set sequence in which the tools may be applied, nor is there any assumption that all the tools will be needed for every job. The analyst must choose whatever methods of study are appropriate and must be aware of the strengths, difficulties of use and defects which each possesses. Having studied the system the findings need to be recorded for further study and to allow the findings to be communicated with ease.

A useful distinction can be made between study of the system at a physical level and its study at a logical level. Study at a physical level focuses on what is being done and how it is done; it will review all the processes, personnel, stationery, files and other materials which may be used. Study at a logical level considers only how a process is done – the rules and procedures by which an input of information is transformed into an output. Which level is chosen will depend very much on the nature of the problem or opportunity, the exploration of which has resulted in the study being carried out. In the case of an opportunity or problem occurring in a system which is isolated from the remainder of the organization it is feasible to consider only the logic of what is being done. If there are no transactions with the other systems, no output to other systems or input from other systems, and the physical nature of the process is simple, then a logical description may be sufficient for the use of a system designer. This is, however, rarely the case and the temptation to ignore the physical aspects of a system should be avoided. At the very least, an examination of the system at a physical level will often reveal areas where one system has links with another and thus where any redesign in one might have an effect on the other system. Also, the problems of implementation can be greatly eased if the design team is aware of the physical differences in the processes to which users may have to become accustomed. Training needs can often be identified by this consideration.

Many of the techniques involve discussing the nature of jobs; personal information may be gathered or opinions about aspects of the work of the organization may be offered. It is important that the analyst make clear to what extent the source of such information will be treated as confidential *before* it is collected. This is a vital step if trust in the analyst is to be maintained.

The fact-finding techniques of questionnaires, interviews and observation will now be outlined, followed by methods of system description.

Questionnaires

The questionnaire is a method of fact finding best suited to circumstances in which the analyst is dealing with an organization having a large and dispersed staff or in which an initial, overall view of a system is needed. Once the questionnaire has been designed, its administration will take little time; it is an economic way of gathering data provided sufficient usable replies are received.

An inadequate response can be attributed to either, or both, of two factors. In the first place, the rate of return of the questionnaire may be low. This is a frequent problem with questionnaires sent through the mail or distributed in bulk. The reason is most likely to be a lack of commitment by the group being surveyed. When dealing with a group of staff, particularly the fairly close-knit community likely to be found in a library or information service, the analyst can help to build up commitment by explaining the purpose of the survey and how the information supplied may enhance the design of a new system to the greater benefit of the staff. In addition, the management can already have assisted the development of commitment by making sure that the project has been openly discussed and staff have been kept informed. Any notion of compulsion is quite wrong: the purpose of explanation is not to impress with authority but, rather, to create a sense of involvement.

There is a greater problem when the survey is to include members from other stakeholder groups, including users. The link between the library or information service and the stakeholder groups may be quite limited, at least in the minds of group members. There may be some opportunity for the analyst to call a meeting to explain the purpose of the survey but full attendance is most unlikely and in the case of a large community of users, such as that of a public library, the calling of a meeting is improbable. Instead, the analyst must rely on other methods, notably publicity, to explain the purpose and importance of the study and to seek cooperation. Discreet moral pressure is sometimes tried. Postal questionnaires may include a reply-paid, addressed, envelope; a ballpoint pen or pencil may be included. The aim is to remove reasons for putting off completing the questionnaire. The ideal is to encourage its completion immediately on receipt. Follow-up letters, which should include another copy of the questionnaire, may be tried but rarely yield many additional replies. In a small group a personal visit is often the most effective way of encouraging completion but takes a lot of time. It may, however, prove quite effective if the visit is combined with other fact-finding work such as interviews or observation.

The other factor which may lead to an inadequate response to a questionnaire is wording which is misunderstood. The problem is acute: it is said, with some justice, that if a question can be misinterpreted, it will be. It is surprisingly difficult to phrase a question unambiguously, especially if it will be read by a large and varied group. The best that can be done is to adhere to a few guidelines and to 'pilot' any questionnaire by asking a few members of the target survey group to cooperate by completing it as a test run and then discussing with them their reactions, misunderstandings and feelings about the questions. Pilot studies are the most effective means of 'trapping' sources of error.

The guidelines which may assist in drawing up a questionnaire are fairly simple. First, make sure that questions are short: if the subject matter is complicated, try to break it into segments so the respondent can answer a question and then move on to the next phase of the argument. Next, ensure that questions use terms appropriate to the user group. Avoiding jargon is often quite difficult because one may be so familiar with the use of a term that it is no longer seen as jargon: for example, 'document' is sometimes used in professional circles to describe any item reproduced on paper, whereas a library user may interpret it to exclude books or journal articles. Even the term 'book' may be understood in different ways. Where there is a possibility of doubt, give examples. At the other end of the spectrum, if there is a professional jargon appropriate to a user group and the analyst is confident that all members will understand it in the same way, there is little point in avoiding it: for example, providing a definition of 'AACR2' is likely to prove irksome to a group of professional cataloguers!

Another guideline is to beware of relying on the accuracy of memory of respondents. It is very difficult to recall clearly what has happened in a previous year or even in the previous month; wherever possible, this type of historical data should be collected by inspection of statistics and other records.

Questionnaires designed as part of a systems analysis are best suited to a preliminary assessment of opinions and feelings, recent events and simple descriptions of processes. Different types of question may be appropriate and may be mixed in the same questionnaire.

Scaled questions ask for a response within a defined category, often by ringing a number on the scale. For example:

My general impression of the library staff is that they

are not very interested in users   are very interested in users

---

1   2   3   4   5   6   7

In designing a scale, it is sometimes suggested that there should be no middle point, the argument being that the respondent should be forced to decide in favour of, or against, the proposition rather than mechanically ticking the mid point of the scale. Some respondents may resent this, however, and draw in a mid-point. There seems little reason to deprive the person with a 'middle-of-the-road' opinion and the dangers of 'mechanical' answering can be avoided if scales are presented so that there is some variety about which end of the scale represents the 'good' or 'high' end.

Scaled questions are closed: that is, the respondent is forced to choose a category already defined by the analyst. Another type of closed question is represented by the 'tick a box' variety:

My length of continuous work experience with this library service is:

less than twelve months   _____
between twelve and fifteen months   _____
greater than fifteen months   _____

The selection of appropriate ranges for the categories must depend on some prior knowledge of the user group. For example, if the question about length of service were used in a department where the staff turnover was low, most respondents might select the 'greater than fifteen months' option and the value of the result would be diminished.

The advantages of closed questions include simplicity of completion and analysis but they may not elicit useful information which does not fall precisely within the categories. Open questions usually ask the respondent to write an opinion without forcing the response:

Please list the duties you normally carry out on a Friday.
....
....
....

It is important to provide sufficient space for a full response: there is a tendency by respondents to restrict an answer if the space is small. Once again, some prior knowledge of the expected range and length of answers is needed.

Open questions can provide beneficial insights but the analyst should balance their use against the additional burden of analysis.

Questions which ask the respondent to rank attributes can be open or closed. An example of an open, ranking, question is:

Which catalogues do you use? Please list them in order of their usefulness to you.

1.
2.
3.
4.

or I don't use the catalogues _____

An example of a closed, ranking, question is:

Below are listed some ways in which the new cataloguing system might benefit you. Please rank them in order of importance to you, assigning the rank '1' to the most important and ending with '4' for the least important.

Ranking

Reducing errors in the catalogue entries
Making searching faster
Making it easier to find information
Making searching more interesting

Presentation is important. Many questionnaires are too long, with the result that they are put aside, with good intention, to be dealt with later. Few are returned. A short, simple, design is a desirable aim.

The preamble to the questionnaire should briefly explain its purpose and to what use the information will be put. If the information includes personal details and is to be stored as part of a computer file this should be clearly stated to ensure that part of the requirements of the Data Protection Act (1984) are satisfied. The name, title and contact address of both the organization responsible for the questionnaire and a contact from whom further information and clarification can be obtained should be given, together with a return address and a closing date for replies.

It is worth spending time on questionnaire design; sources such as Heather and Stone,[1] Line[2] or Hoinville and Jowell[3] will provide useful guidance.

Interviews

Talking to people is the main way in which analysts gather information. An interview may be thought of as being a structured discussion, the analyst having prepared quite carefully for the encounter. This is not to suggest that it need be formal or tightly controlled: rather, it means that the analyst has decided what information it would be useful to obtain and in what way the interviewee can help in providing that information. Interviews in the early stages of fact finding are often exploratory and relatively free of structure, the aim being for the analyst to gain a broad knowledge of a process or function of part of the organization. In later stages, interviews can be used to gather facts and opinions, to verify information gained from other sources and to explore problems such as resistance to change.

Planning of interviews begins with the definition of the purpose of the interview, followed by a careful gathering of background information about the nature of the jobs undertaken by intended respondents. Armed with this information, the analyst is able to discuss matters with an evident degree of knowledge and thus gain the confidence of respondents.

The planning of interviews should include preparation of the interviewee: every effort should be made to set the interviewee at ease. Permission for the interview to take place may have to be sought from a departmental head: the terms of reference should indicate whether or not direct approaches to staff are permitted. In any case, it is usually wise to ensure that senior management are made aware of which members of staff are likely to be asked, and when, to reduce the possibility of clashes with other duties. If possible, and if the facilities are suitable, the analyst should conduct the interview at the location where the interviewee works. Familiar surroundings help a person settle down and relax.

An interview is an exercise in interpersonal behaviour and success depends upon the analyst and the interviewee responding to each other in an appropriate way. Jenkins and Johnson[4] have reviewed the importance of body language in the conduct of interviews. As well as the analyst observing the respondent for signs of tension, boredom and so on, it is important that analysts be aware of how their own body language may affect the respondents. Folded arms, for example, may indicate a defensive posture; open arms, may indicate a receptive attitude. Maintaining frequent eye contact can indicate interest, though care must be taken not to stare since this tends to be interpreted as a threat.

The analyst must try to be impartial; as mentioned in chapter 2, there is a danger that the analyst will be perceived either as enemy or fellow conspirator unless a neutral standpoint is confidently maintained. This may require tact and the ability to steer a participant back to the matter in hand. An analyst must, above all, be a good listener and this is especially true when interviewing.

The analyst should be careful to adjust the level of formality to suit the circumstances: first impressions will be very important and matters such as inappropriate dress, appearance or manner can prejudice the success of the interview. Neutrality is the aim. It is also important to consider seating arrangements: placing the analyst behind a desk will project an image of authority which may intimidate or annoy.

On the other hand, the analyst must appear business-like and clear in leading the interviewee through the stages of discussion. One device for achieving this is to use a 'structured' interview where the discussion is governed by the completion of a questionnaire. A modified approach is offered by the 'semi-structured' interview. This technique allows the analyst to decide in advance what information is needed using a questionnaire as a guide, with the advantage that potentially interesting responses can be followed up immediately and additional information can be gathered. Both types produce sets of standardized, or partly standardized, responses which can then be compared and aggregated. Unstructured interviews follow no predetermined script apart from an initial outline by the analyst of the reasons for the interview. Such interviews can provide valuable data but the technique requires a lot of time. Its virtue is that it offers a way of exploring ideas quite deeply and does not constrain the respondent. It would be appropriate, for example, as a means of exploring the attitude of some users to a service where there is little prior knowledge of their background and needs.

Constructing the interview 'script' for a structured or semi-structured interview requires the same considerations as already outlined for questionnaire construction, with one additional point. There is ample research evidence that using slightly different orders of words, different emphasis or even tone of voice, will influence the responses and thus introduce substantial bias. In a thorough study of the problem in relation to social research, Belson[5] has indicated that it is subtle in its effects and quite difficult to control. Although one could argue that the effects would be less serious in the smaller environments of a systems study and project development the general proposition that validity (that is, the ability of a measure to measure accurately what it is supposed to measure) cannot be assumed and some care must be taken by the analyst if comparisons of the views of respondents are to be made.

Semi-structured interviews will, by their nature, involve a freer discussion with participants. A good interviewer will try to distinguish between opinion and fact but will remember that it may be important to note that a particular opinion is held even though there may be no evidence to support the opinion. In dealing with resistance to change, for example, a firm knowledge of what opinions are held is a first step towards understanding the reason for the resistance and coping with its effects. To set a person's opinion aside as being wrong or irrelevant is to forget that the person must, at some stage, be encouraged to change the opinion. It is also wise to be wary of praising something which may have to be changed and of condemning features of the existing system.

Keeping an accurate record of interviews can be quite difficult, except for structured interviews where the questionnaire will form the record. Another useful technique is structured note-taking, a method explained by Buzan.[6] The record takes the form of a diagram consisting of lines emerging from a central point with the various arguments and responses being recorded briefly on the lines (Figure 12). The technique is quick to use and can serve as a good memory aid when a fuller, written, record of the interview is later made.

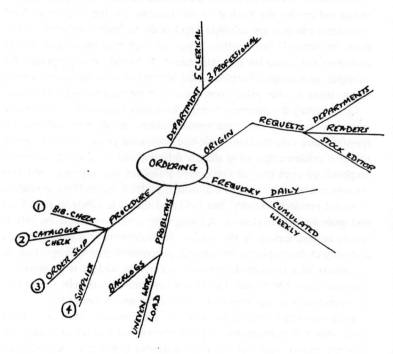

Figure 12   Structured note-taking

Tape recording is the best method of creating a record of an unstructured interview: the record of the discussion is complete and the full attention of the analyst can be given to the respondent. On the other hand, microphone shyness may inhibit the conversation. For this reason, the covert use of a recorder has sometimes been suggested; this, however, is ethically dubious and would certainly cause a loss of trust in the analyst if it were later to be discovered.

At the end of an interview it is helpful if the analyst summarizes the discussion, to check that comments made have been understood, and then invites the participant to respond. This is another key point where the analyst should listen very carefully because the respondent will often be prompted to supply additional information and corrections.

So far, the assumption has been that one-to-one interviews are being conducted. There is no reason why the techniques of the semi-structured and the unstructured interviews should not be extended to group interviews. The interactions between respondents are likely to enrich the data collected but this must be balanced by the additional difficulties of recording the results. As mentioned in chapter 2, tape recording may not be the easy solution it might seem. Another possibility to consider is the use of a second analyst to act as reporter.

An alternative to face-to-face interviewing is the use of the telephone. This is generally not as satisfactory as face-to-face interviewing because of the absence of body language and the consequent difficulty of building up an empathy between analyst and respondent. It is useful, though, as a means of follow-up or for clarifying points arising from an earlier face-to-face interview.

Useful guides to interview techniques are given by Stone[7] and Moser and Kalton.[8]

Observation

Another fact-finding technique which is of considerable use to the analyst is that of observation. Use of the technique allows the analyst to see how a job is done, to gain direct knowledge of the problems and bottlenecks and to make some estimate of workloads, processing speeds and so on.

Observation can be structured: the analyst can prepare a list of activities, perhaps as a result of a prior interview, and then collect data on the frequency of their occurrence, duration of activity and outcome. For example, a study might be made of the range of enquiries received at an enquiry desk in a library: the analyst may already have decided that it would be sensible to distinguish between various types of enquiry and have designed a form to allow the enquiries to be categorized. At the times nominated for the survey, the analyst could observe the desk and count and categorize the enquiries.

Semi-structured observation is also possible. The analyst can conduct what is sometimes called a 'walk-through' by starting at the beginning of a process and following the sequence of events, observing and measuring at each significant stage. The aim is to record, in some detail, the complete process and to distinguish links with other processes. Once again some prior knowledge of the general work of the organization is needed if the information gathered is to form any coherent picture. For example, following several books through the process of cataloguing would reveal the stages, what files and other sources of information (catalogue codes, etc.) are consulted and what information is eventually produced. Some estimates of time for each stage could also be made and any evident delays or slack periods noted. Semi-structured observation also offers an opportunity for checking facts and impressions gathered by the use of interviews or questionnaires and for following up the loose ends or occasional inconsistencies which emerge when people describe their jobs. The analyst must be alert to the fact that a respondent may well take for granted certain aspects of the job which will be of importance to the system study: for example, mention of a special procedure which is only used on rare occasions may well have been omitted during the description of a job in an interview. Observing the job gives the analyst the opportunity to check systematically at each stage that procedures appropriate to every contingency have been described.

Although unstructured observation is an unlikely concept within the context of a system study, it can exist where the analyst has ready access to the workplace and, by chance, happens to notice something of interest. Such observation is unsystematic and unplanned but it is often the source of important and unsuspected information which may then form the basis for a more structured enquiry. It is important for the analyst to be alert to every opportunity to observe.

Observation can include the study of the records kept by the organization. As a process is observed, examples of forms used can be gathered, including some which have been completed to show the types of information recorded. Statistics can be studied to identify peaks and troughs in demand for processes. Procedure manuals may be checked to provide detailed job descriptions. Organization charts can be viewed to gain an overall picture of the structure and lines of authority in the organization. This information will need to be checked because manuals and charts tend to record the 'official' view, or an historical view, which is no longer representative of working practice. The study of records can form the basis for further enquiries during interviews or as part of a 'walk-through'. In particular, it will be helpful to make some assessment about how useful the various forms and records are; clearly, the workers who use them are best placed to offer an opinion.

So far it has been assumed that the analyst will be a 'participant observer': the analyst will work within a group or with an individual, asking questions and watching what is happening. In this role the analyst is in an excellent position to seek clarification, to check observations and to gain an insider's view. Interpersonal behaviour will have an important effect on the quality of the observations and the analyst must be aware of the importance of behaving in a way which sets those being observed at ease. Social skills are very necessary if observation is to be a comfortable process for both parties. As with questionnaires and interviews, why the observation is taking place should be clearly explained and any necessary permission sought.

'Non-participant' observation is also possible: here, the observer looks on passively and does not interact with those being observed. This is almost always rather disturbing, even if the reasons for the observation are clear, and those being observed may become tense with consequent effects on their behaviour. On balance, there is more to be gained by participant observation.

Covert observation has sometimes been suggested as a means of gathering information when it is thought that the acknowledged presence of an observer may lead to atypical behaviour. For example, it may be necessary to discover for how long users persist in searching in a manual catalogue. Experience may suggest that users under overt observation do not search as they might if unobserved: in an attempt to please the observer they may, for example, rationalize their searching process and persist for far longer than normal. Covert observation could provide more accurate evidence of the typical durations of searches. It is, however, very difficult to arrange for such a procedure in the context of libraries and information services and there are ethical objections as well.

Recording observations can be quite tedious and the analyst needs to consider carefully what form the record should take to ensure that it can be made quickly and without interfering with the process of observation. Photocopies of procedure manuals and other documents, copies of forms and other material encountered during observation should be obtained wherever possible. A log, perhaps based on the structured note-taking

95

described in the previous section, is often used and personal tape recorders can provide a quick means of recording impressions. There is no substitute, however, for the writing up of a full report, preferably as soon as possible after the observation has taken place. Memory soon fades and important details can become quite obscure after even a short delay.

A variant which may be helpful, especially for analysing the work of senior managers, is the diary, a form of self-observation. The participant is asked to enter details of events specified by the analyst. For example, a manager might be asked to record the points at which financial data are used during the working day. The record may have to be quite full: to continue the example, the source of the financial data and the use to which they are to be put might also need to be recorded. The burden of recording can be considerable and participants may forget to make entries or fill in the diary, with varying degrees of accuracy, at the end of the day, so it is a technique best confined to a short period. Nevertheless, such studies can provide very useful information.

Another variant is the failure study. This focuses on problems arising in a process and aims to identify the reasons for failure. For example, in designing an online public access catalogue (OPAC) it would be of considerable benefit to know why some searches carried out in the existing catalogue appear to fail. A large number of searches would need to be observed and some criterion for declaring a search to be a success or a failure would need to be defined. Each designated failure could then be studied to discover if the failure could be attributed to faulty information supplied by the searcher or failure by the information retrieval system to respond to correct information. In the early stages, the technique needs the cooperation of the participant to supply details of what process is being undertaken (in the given example, details of the information brought to the search and the search strategies adopted) and the results. Thereafter, the study of a failure is undertaken by the analyst. Considerable time and ingenuity may be required to explain the range of failures but the information obtained is of great value.

An excellent guide to observation is given by Mullings.[9]

Census or sample?
In conducting a systems analysis of a small library or information service, one that has few staff, it may be quite possible to interview, observe or administer questionnaires to all members of staff in the same category, thus carrying out a type of census. If the systems analysis is concerned

with the cataloguing system then it may be possible to survey all the cataloguers. There is some benefit in this because there is less likelihood of important information being overlooked or forgotten, there is an opportunity to check observations with all members of the group and a total picture of the work of the group can be built up. In addition there is the benefit which can accrue from the sense of involvement which every member of the group will have a chance to develop. On the other hand, costs can be quite high and there may be a lot of repetition of well-established facts. The novelty value of the extra information which might be gained may not be so great as to offset the expenditure of resources.

If the group is very large or dispersed over a wide geographic area (for example, a county library service) or if it is somewhat amorphous and outside the direct control of the organization (for example, users of a public library) then recourse to sampling will be necessary.

There is always a limit to the accuracy of the information derived from a sample. The aim of any survey is to describe some characteristics of a group, or 'population'. A population need not consist of people: it can be objects (books or periodicals, for example), processes (enquiries, for example) or phenomena (accidents or errors, for example). The only way in which a complete description of the characteristics for the population can be developed is for all members to be surveyed: in other words, to carry out a census. The procedure for carrying out a sample survey involves measuring the characteristics as seen in part of the group and then, by inference, ascribing the measure to the whole group. Since there is always a risk that the sub-group will not completely represent the characteristic, it is common practice to report results within a range of possibilities. For example, the mean length of loans of books from a library might be reported as:

15.3 days $\pm$ 0.2 days at 95% confidence

This means that the variability of the data from the sample suggests that the true mean for the population lies somewhere between 15.1 days and 15.5 days and that this estimate is likely to be correct in 95 cases out of 100. In other words, there is a risk that the estimate may be wrong and it is for the analyst and management to consider how big a risk can be tolerated. In many circumstances, the consequences of being wrong may be quite trivial, provided the estimate is not too wide of the true figure. In other cases, the success of a project may depend on the estimate being correct. A larger sample will usually yield a closer estimate and one that may be given with, perhaps, 99% confidence. Using a larger

97

sample will cost more so it is necessary for the additional costs to be balanced against the need for accuracy. In circumstances where the inherent variability of the population is unknown it may be necessary to conduct a pilot study to ascertain this.

It is evident that selection of a sample is a crucial step if the measures derived from the sample are to be representative of the population. Statistical sampling theory is a complicated topic and the decision about how to carry out a major survey should best be taken in consultation with an expert statistician. Help should also be sought if the accuracy of the results of the survey will be critical to the success of the project. In the circumstances of many system studies a limited range of information is needed and a high level of accuracy is not critical, though major errors are clearly undesirable.

Random sampling is the basis for creating representative sample groups. The essence of random sampling is to ensure that every member of the population has an equal chance of being included in the sample. Simple random sampling requires that each member of the population be numbered, the sample then being chosen by picking numbers from a table of random numbers. Stratified random sampling is used in cases where the population consists of distinct groups and where there is some reason to suppose that the characteristics of the groups are important for the study. For example, in assessing the attitude of users to readers for microforms, age may be a significant factor. To ensure that the sample fairly represents all ages, the population is divided into age groups and a simple random sample can be chosen from each group, its size being dependent on the proportion of the population included in that group. If 30% of the parent population are placed in an age group of 50 to 59 years then the overall sample should include 30% who are in this group.

Several of the textbooks already mentioned contain detailed studies of sampling techniques. A useful overview is given by Stone and Harris.[10] Thorough coverage of the topic is given by Simpson[11] and Swisher and McClure.[12]

Documentation and charts

Any systems study will result in the gathering of a large amount of information, including documents, specimen forms, written statements, statistics and other data. Unless the analyst establishes, from the beginning, good procedures for recording, storing and cross-referencing this information, much will be lost or overlooked. Good standardized documentation is a help in preventing this. The National Computing

Centre (NCC) has developed in its data processing documentation standards[13] a range of standard forms and conventions which can be of use in a somewhat wider range of circumstances than computer applications design. Each form type is named and also carries boxes for title, identification and other codes, date of compilation and author, thus allowing a comprehensive description of a system to be built up over several linked sheets. The forms for 'system outline' (Figure 13), 'chart sheet' (Figure 14) and 'clerical document specification' (Figure 15) are especially useful and can suit most needs at this level of analysis. The 'chart sheet', in particular, can be used to record a variety of information, including organization charts and flowcharts. The 'system outline' is a good means of recording the main components in a system and indicating the reference of the chart, giving more detailed information about individual components.

A flowchart is a useful means of describing a process or recording a sequence of events. It is possible to describe a simple process in words but complicated processes may require many pages of description and if there are several options or alternative procedures the description may become very difficult to follow. A flowchart can also serve as an excellent means of communication and a record of the analysis. The drawing of a flowchart can also identify points where the analyst's information is incomplete or possibly inaccurate.

Several flowcharting conventions have been developed to suit the needs of work-study engineers, computer software producers and other specialists. For the purpose of a systems analysis study at a general level, especially if it is to be undertaken by analysts who are not specialists, the procedure flowcharting convention will usually prove the most useful. A procedure flowchart consists of a network of boxes, each of which contains a brief description of part of the process. Lines are used to connect the boxes, with arrows showing the direction of flow. Distinctive shapes are used to represent facets of the process. Figure 16 shows the range of symbols recommended in the NCC data processing documentation standards; in practice, the description of quite complex procedures can be accomplished using a limited range: the 'process' rectangle, diamond 'decision' box, input/output parallelogram, round-ended terminator symbol, flowlines and the connectors. The other symbols are used in drawing the more specialized charts required for specifying computer software routines.

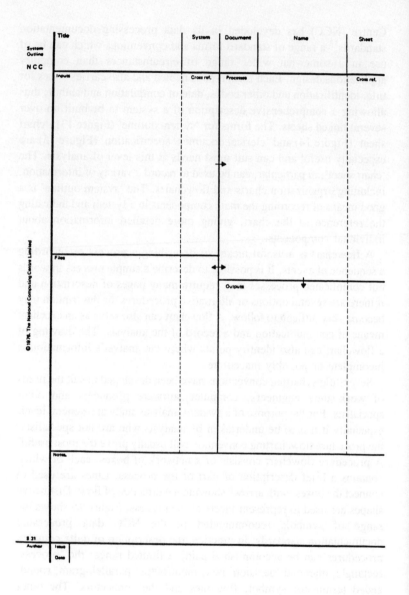

Figure 13   NCC system outline chart

100

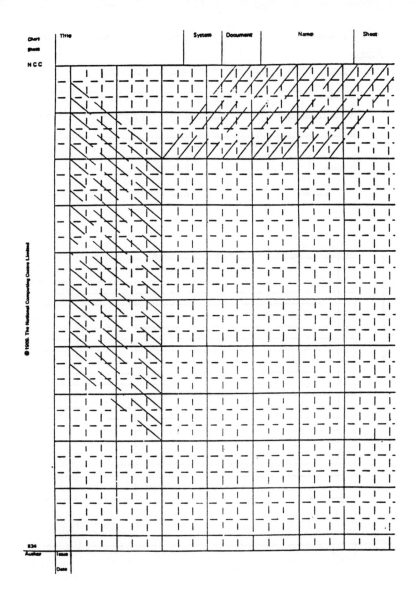

Figure 14   NCC chart sheet

101

Clerical Document Specification

NCC

Document description		System	Document	Name	Sheet

Stationery ref.	Size		Number of parts	Method of preparation

Filing sequence	Medium	Prepared/maintained by

Frequency of preparation/update	Retention period	Location

	Minimum	Maximum	Av/Abs	Growth rate/fluctuations
VOLUME				

Users/recipients	Purpose	Frequency of use

Ref.	Item	Picture	Occurrence	Value range	Source of data

Notes

S 41

Author	Issue
	Date

Figure 15   NCC clerical document specification

102

Symbol / Type of Chart	System Flowchart Interactive System Flowchart and Clerical Procedure Flowchart	Computer Run Chart	Computer Procedure Flowchart
1 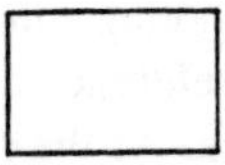 ▭	All operations or procedures		
2 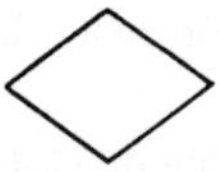 ◇	All decisions		
3 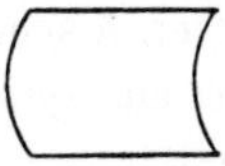 (storage symbol)	Storage media, permanent or temporary	Computer Backing Storage	Not used
4 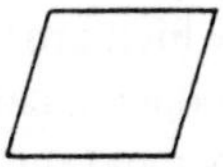 ▱	Documents, cards, paper tape, displays, etc.	Data passing between computer and non-computer parts of the system	Not used
5 ◯	Connector, showing continuity between symbols where it is not possible to join them by a flowline		
6  (terminator)	Terminator, showing entry to or exit from a procedure		
7  ▽ ▷	Data moving from one location to another	Not used	

Figure 16   NCC flowchart symbols

103

There is a temptation to build up complex charts on large sheets of paper. These look impressive but are always difficult to understand and may serve to obscure rather than reveal stages of a process. It is best to develop simple charts with a restricted range of symbols. If a complex process is to be described this can be achieved by a hierarchy of charts. The topmost chart should deal with the process at a general level, (or even be used to outline the complete system) each box denoting a major stage; a stripe at the top of the box should contain the reference code for the chart giving the next level of detail for that stage. At the next level each major stage is expanded into a separate chart. It is possible to extend this idea through several levels, each subordinate level expanding a stage from the next higher level.

Numbering each symbol is a major help if, in subsequent reports, attention has to be drawn to a particular stage on a chart. The numbering should run sequentially from 1, starting afresh with each sheet. A symbol can thus be identified uniquely by a combination of sheet and symbol number: 2.9 would be symbol 9 on sheet 2, for example.

Arranging the chart so that the major flow is down the page or left-to-right assists the reader. Avoid creating lots of flowlines which cross or flow back to earlier stages: the use of connectors will produce a neater appearance. Each connector should include the sheet number and symbol from which it emerges or to which it links. Figure 17 illustrates a procedure chart for a simple process.

Most processes include the making of decisions. If there are many decisions associated with a process, the resultant flowchart can become very difficult to follow and it may be best to replace part of the flowchart by an alternative presentation: the decision table. Each table is given a descriptive title. The table is divided into four. The upper quadrants describe the conditions associated with a decision, the lower quadrants describe actions (Figure 18). To the left are recorded descriptions, (this area of the table is often called the 'stub') whilst to the right (often called the 'entries' area) are listed the rules for making the decision. The number of lines and columns can be ruled to suit individual needs.

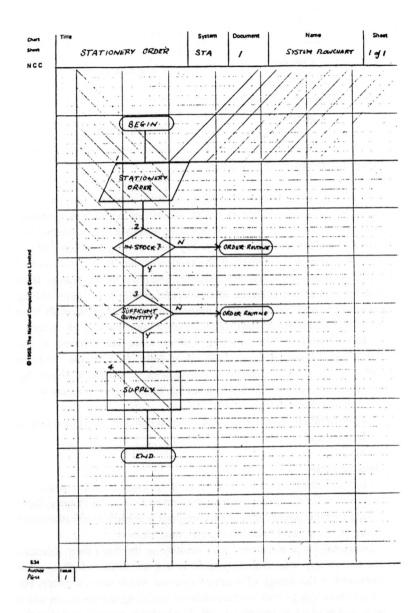

BEGIN

STATIONERY ORDER

2
IN-STOCK ? — N → ORDER ROUTINE

Y

3
SUFFICIENT QUANTITY ? — N → ORDER ROUTINE

Y

4
SUPPLY

END

© 1963. The National Computing Centre Limited

S34

Author Issue
PGu   1

Figure 17   Flowchart

105

	Rules
Condition stub	Condition entries
Action stub	Action entries

Figure 18 Decision table structure

To illustrate the use of the decision table, consider the following example. An academic library has an acquisition policy which permits any category of reader to suggest items for purchase. Titles costing less than £10 are ordered immediately. For titles costing between £10 and £19, the order is immediate if the request comes from a member of academic staff or a research student; requests in this range from undergraduates are referred to a selection committee. Items costing between £20 and £49 are ordered immediately if the request comes from a member of academic staff; requests from other sources are referred to the committee. Items costing £50 or more are referred to the committee. Figure 19 shows the decision table. A 'Y' in the condition entries quadrant shows that a condition applies, whilst an 'N' shows that the condition is not satisfied. An 'X' in the 'action' entry quadrant shows that a particular action is carried out.

Documentation, flowcharting and decision tables are discussed further by Daniels and Yeates.[14]

Data analysis

So far, this discussion of the analysis of systems has concentrated on the physical level. As mentioned in the first section in this chapter, there is a logical level which, although its presence is implicit in any discussion of the physical level, needs separate consideration.

Data analysis is concerned with identifying the data, their structure and use in any information system. It is a technique which is often employed in the design of database systems which use computers but the technique can provide useful insights in analysing any system in which information plays an important part. The technique serves to define the types of things to which the organization needs access if it is to function and what it needs to know about these things. In particular, where

	1	2	3	4	5	6	7	8
Cost : less than £10	Y	N	N	N	N	N	N	N
Cost : £10-£19.99	-	Y	Y	Y	N	N	N	N
Cost : £20-£49.99	-	-	-	-	Y	Y	Y	N
Cost : over £50	-	-	-	-	-	-	-	Y
Requester : undergraduate	-	N	N	Y	N	N	Y	-
Requester : research student	-	N	Y	N	N	Y	N	-
Requester : academic staff	-	Y	N	N	Y	N	N	-
Immediate purchase	X	X	X		X			
Selection committee				X		X	X	X

Figure 19 Decision table example

information is passed from one system, or subsystem to another it is important that the structure of the data facilitates this exchange. Thus, a knowledge of the data structure is vital.

A starting point is the 'data dictionary'. During the investigation of a system a lot of information about the data used in the system will have been obtained. In observing processes, or listening to descriptions of processes, the analyst will have discovered what data is created or used, its origin and how it is linked to other processes. The data dictionary provides a record of all the data which is known to exist in the system. In its simplest form, it can be a manual file, based on a standard form such as the NCC Clerical document specification, and should record:

- *name* of data item (e.g. 'price', 'date') with any alternative names used;
- *'picture'*, giving its composition and size in alphanumeric characters, if it can be defined. A date, for example, might consist of four numeric characters (often shown as '9(4)') for year only or a mixture of alphabetic and numeric characters if the day and month are to be included (for example, '99AAAA9999'). In contrast, some data items (for example, titles of books) are inherently variable in composition and size and thus cannot be confined to a set 'picture';
- *range*, if definable. A valid accession number might, for a particular

107

departmental collection in a library system, always consist of 6 numeric characters in the range 100000 to 400000. Some data items will obviously vary in length and cannot thus be confined to a set range;

● *origin* — there may be several possible sources. For example, information about the price of a book may be supplied by a user, discovered from a trade bibliography, database held on CD-ROM, publisher's circular and so on. Some data items may have their origins in other processes: for example, the title of a newly acquired book may be passed from the acquisitions to the cataloguing process;

● *uses* — the processes in which it appears as a component part; how it is *stored* — both its logical position within other records and physically as part of a paper file, for example;

● *volume* — how many data items of this type will be generated per unit of time; whether this volume is static or growing and, if so, at what rate;

● *security aspects* — is access to the data item restricted in any way? For example, access to the names and addresses of library users might be restricted to members of library staff; in a commercial information service, access to some company financial or product data might be restricted to certain categories of company staff;

● *other comments*.

Another facet of data analysis is the creation of a data model. The purpose of data modelling is to facilitate an understanding of how data is used by an organization. There are many suggested ways in which this may be done, most of which are intended for the computer specialist. Veryard [15] has produced a guide which is simple and not restricted to discussing information systems which depend on computers.

A data model may be built up from three components:

● *entities*: any object (real or conceptual) about which it is possible to gather data — users, books, requests are examples. It may be possible to identify classes, or types, of entities as well as occurrences of individuals. For example, it would be possible to identify library staff as an entity but recognize the Librarian in charge of Reference Services as an individual;

● *relationships*: entities are linked to each other through relationships, or the effect that one has on another. Thus, the Librarian in charge of Reference Services is manager of the staff of the Reference Library, where 'is manager of' denotes the relationship and its direction.

108

Relationships may be long term or transient: a book is borrowed by a user for only a short time, for example;
- *attributes*: the data which describes the entity is termed an 'attribute'. A number of attributes may be attached to an entity type. For example, for the entity type 'user', the attributes 'name', 'address', 'reader number' might be stored. For each occurrence of the entity 'user', the attributes will have particular values, such as 'John Smith', '3 The Lane, Uplands, Upshire' and '1232456'. In order to identify any entity occurrence uniquely there must be an attribute which it alone possesses. In the example, this could be the 'reader number' because there may be other people called John Smith and there may be several people living at the given address.

Several types of relationship may exist in a data model:

- *one-to-one* − each occurrence of an entity type is related to one occurrence of a second entity type and vice versa. Each accession record can relate to only one book in a library collection and each book can relate to only one accession record, for example;
- *one-to-many* − each occurrence of an entity type is related to several occurrences of second entity type. A catalogue record may relate to several copies of a book, for example;
- *many-to-one* − a 'one-to-many' relationship the other way round. Each occurrence of a second entity type is related to several occurrences of a first entity type. For example, a library user may be a user of only one library at a time but a library may have many users. Between the entity types 'user' and 'library' the relationship 'is member of' represents a many-to-one nature;
- *many-to-many* − an occurrence of a first entity type is related to several occurrences of the second entity type and an occurrence of the second entity type is related to several occurrences of the first entity type. A supplier, for example, may be able to supply many different books and a book may be supplied by many different suppliers;
- *involuted* − occurrences of one entity type are related to occurrences of the same entity type. For the entity type 'staff', there is an involuted relationship because members of the staff will normally work with other members of the staff.

It is usually helpful to draw a diagram to represent the data model. The conventions are simple and shown in Figure 20.

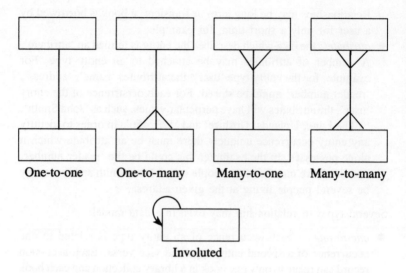

One-to-one   One-to-many   Many-to-one   Many-to-many

Involuted

Figure 20   Data model conventions

As an example of developing a data model, consider this description of a current awareness service, which might have been obtained by interviewing members of staff. The entities are represented in italics.

Documents received by the *library* are scanned by an *information officer*. For any *document* an *abstract* is written by the *information officer*. *Abstracts* are cumulated into a *bulletin original* which is copied. A *bulletin copy* is then sent to each *user* who may then contact the *information officer* to borrow any *documents* drawn to their attention.

The next step is to pair up each entity type and to consider whether a meaningful, direct, and useful relationship can be established between them. There is a direct relationship between documents and the library, for example. It is often helpful to summarize the relationships in the form of a grid and a diagram (Figure 21).

The diagram can then form the basis for discussion because some aspects may have been misunderstood or may be misrepresented. For example, it may be explained that all users do not automatically receive a copy of the bulletin: perhaps it is only distributed to those who ask for it to be sent. In this way, the model, and the analyst's understanding of the work of the organization, may be refined.

110

Entity relationship	Type
1. Documents received by library	M : 1
2. Documents scanned by Information Officer	M : 1
3. Documents yield abstracts	M : M
4. Documents may be of interest to several users	M : M
5. Library employs Information Officer	1 : 1
6. Library has many users	1 : M
7. Information Officer produces many abstracts	1 : M
8. Information Officer is contacted by users	1 : M
9. Abstracts form bulletin original	M : 1
10 Bulletin original reproduced as copies	1 : M
11. Bulletin copy circulated to user	1 : 1

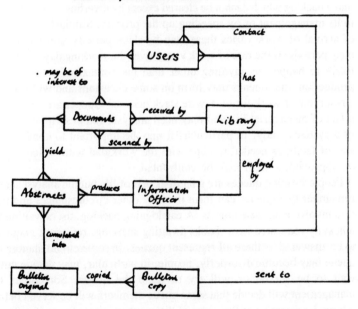

Figure 21 Data model example

111

The subject of data analysis is quite complex but well worth pursuing if processes are to be automated and information is to be held in databases. A readable guide to the approach, particularly in relation to computer applications, is given by Rock-Evans.[16] Avison[17] has described the use of data analysis, including the use of data dictionaries, within the context of information systems development.

Simple queueing theory

Queues are an inherent feature of most systems and a useful means of balancing the flow of work. In any process where work is passed from hand to hand, or process to process, there is the need to balance the desire, on behalf of management, for work to be completed as quickly as possible, commensurate with the need for efficiency, and for full employment of the resources available to do the work. If the rate of work is very high, the resources may stand idle, waiting for a job to arrive; on the other hand, if the work rate is low, a queue may begin and develop into a backlog which cannot be cleared except by diverting extra resources to its management or by speeding up the process. Similarly, if the rate of arrival of work varies there may be slack periods alternating with busy periods. If the rate of work varies over the working day, as is most likely to happen in anything other than the context of an automated production line, queues may form on some occasions and will serve as a reservoir of work for otherwise slack periods. Queues are, therefore, a fact of managerial life and may need analysis and description as part of a systems study. In particular, it may be important to consider the size of facilities needed to cope with the workload with which a new, or improved, system may be confronted.

People forming queues are a familiar part of life but the analyst should remember that queues can form in many other circumstances and may also involve inanimate objects. A cataloguing backlog, users waiting for a heavily requested item; books awaiting shelving, reference enquiries to be answered — these all represent queues. In some circumstances the queue may become disorderly: people, in particular, may decide not to wait to be served or will try to jump the queue. Sometimes the management will decide that some queue members will be served before others, irrespective of the order of their arrival: providing a 'fast track' for reserved books through the cataloguing process, for example. These aspects make the analysis of queueing quite difficult and require a sophisticated approach. There are, however, many circumstances where knowledge of simple queueing theory will provide some useful insights.

Queueing problems revolve around the rate at which customers (people and other entities) can be be dealt with at a service point. In essence, the analyst is concerned with the rate at which a queue can be served and how to balance the number of available service positions with the anticipated customer demand: it is wasteful to hold service positions open if demand is small, but potentially ineffective to have few service points open and long queues.

The development of a simple queueing model depends on knowing several features about the system:

(a) the input to the system — that is, the anticipated interval between customer arrivals;
(b) the number of servers available — these could be human servers or machines;
(c) the queue discipline — that is, in what order customers are served and whether customers can abandon the queue;
(d) the output from the system — that is, how long it takes to serve a customer.

A queueing model can be used to answer several questions. The main questions are, first, what is the average length of a queue? Secondly, what is the average waiting time which a customer might have to endure? Thirdly, from the point of view of the server, what is the average waiting time between customers?

Simple queueing theory relies upon certain conditions being satisfied. In particular, it is assumed that customer arrivals will be random and independent of each other (strictly, the pattern of arrivals should conform to a Poisson probability distribution) and that the duration of service will be independent and conform to a negative exponential distribution. Being 'independent' means that a previous customer arrival or service duration will have no effect on later arrivals or service lengths. Random arrivals means that there is no systematic effect which could lead to a regularity in the arrivals: for example, in an academic library, there may be a large influx of students shortly after the end of a lecture period and this would violate the assumption of random arrivals. A negative exponential distribution of service duration means that there will be many short service durations tailing smoothly down to a small number which are very long.

The other assumptions built into the simple queueing model are that there is only one server and that the queue discipline is 'first come, first served' with no one quitting the queue. The system includes the queue (if there is one), the person being served and the server. The system

113

model is represented by an equation:

Traffic intensity (ρ) = arrival rate (a)/service rate (s)

Both rates must be in the same units: for example, people per hour, books per day. If the value of the traffic intensity exceeds 1, the queue will grow indefinitely because the rate of arrivals is greater than the rate of service. It is customary to denote traffic intensity as 'ρ', arrival rate as 'a' and service rate as 's'.

Other formulae may be derived (no attempt will be made to demonstrate this but a textbook such as Bunday[18] provides the details):

Probability of no customers in system	:	$(1 - \rho)$
Probability of n customers in system	:	$\rho^n (1 - \rho)$
Probability of more than n customers in system	:	$\rho^{(n + 1)}$
Average number of customers in system (N)	:	$\rho / (1 - \rho)$
Average queue length (Q)	:	$\rho^2 / (1 - \rho)$
Average waiting time before service	:	Q / a
Average time spent in system	:	N / a
Probability that customer will have to wait longer than time t for service (where 'e' is the mathematical constant with a value of approximately 2.718)	:	$\rho e^{-t(s-a)}$
Average queue length when there is a queue	:	$1 / (1 - \rho)$

As an example of use, consider the following. A single photocopier has been installed in a library. After some months there are complaints that users are having to wait in a queue for a long time to be served. Before taking any further action, an analyst is asked to investigate. By observation, the analyst discovers that the machine can serve a mean (i.e. an average) value of 20 customers an hour. During a survey period the rate of arrivals is found to be a mean value of 16 an hour and arrivals are randomly distributed. What is the probability that a customer will have to wait to use the machine and what is the expected length of the queue?

Arrival rate (a) = 16 customers an hour
Service rate (s) = 20 customers an hour
∴traffic intensity (ρ) = a / s = 16 / 20 = 0.8
Since ρ is less than 1, the queue will *not* grow indefinitely.

Having to wait to use the machine means that there must be at least one person in the system at the time of arrival; but,

probability of there being no customers in the system
$$= (1 - \rho) = (1 - 0.8) = 0.2$$
so, the probability of there being a queue is 0.8.
(there can be no other possibilities – either there *is* a queue or there
is *not*, so the sum of the probabilities must be 1).

An alternative method is to ask: what is the probability of there being
more than 0 customers in the system at the time of arrival? This is
determined by evaluating the expression $\rho^{(n+1)}$ with n set to the value 0:

$$\rho^{(n+1)} = 0.8^{(0+1)} = 0.8^1 = 0.8$$

The average queue length is determined using the appropriate formula:

$$\rho^2 / (1 - \rho) = 0.8^2 / (1 - 0.8) = 0.64 / 0.2 = 3.2.$$

So, on average, a customer will find that in 8 cases out of 10 there
will be a queue on arrival and the average length will be about 3
customers. The management would now have to consider whether the
service needed augmenting to cope with this level of demand.

Queueing models of greater complexity have been thoroughly explored
by Morse.[19]

Simulation

There are many problems associated with the management of systems
which are too complicated for analytical techniques such as simple
queueing theory. This is because many real systems involve a large
number of interacting factors, the relationship between which may not
be clear. In addition, the outcomes from a system may be probabilistic
rather than deterministic. With a deterministic system, an input of a
certain kind can be guaranteed to yield an output of a certain kind because
the system has been designed for this. In a probabilistic system, an input
can yield one of a number of possible outputs, some being more likely
than others. In other words, there is no 'mechanical' link between input
and output.

The systems in libraries and information services often conform to
the probabilistic pattern. For example, in a library with a loan period
of 10 days, if a user borrows a book, there is clearly no certainty that
it will be returned after exactly 10 days; rather, based on previous
experience of the borrowing habits of the user group, an analyst could
show that there are varying probabilities for it being returned from within
one day and up to 10 or more days. There is also a probability that it

will never be returned or that it will meet with one of those extraordinary accidents, the details of which often enliven issue desk conversations.

Creating models of such systems is possible but requires some sophisticated mathematics. It is sometimes possible, however, to use past events to gain insight into how a system is operating and to speculate on what might happen if the system were to be redesigned. This technique of 'simulation' is also useful if dealing with circumstances where the assumptions built into simpler methods of analysis cannot be met. For example, simple queueing theory cannot be applied where there is more than one service point or where the rate of arrivals is non-random. In these cases, simulation can offer a fairly simple method of analysis.

To illustrate the technique, consider again the problem of the photo-copier. Suppose the analyst has noticed that the rate of arrivals is not, as had been thought, randomly distributed but is, instead, bunched so that there is a greater likelihood of a queue soon after opening than at other times during the day. It may be worth considering this period as being special and distinct from the remainder of the day. The analyst conducts a short survey on a particular day and records the time of arrival of each user and how long each user takes to use the photocopier. The queue discipline is observed to be 'first come, first served' and nobody abandoned the queue. Over a half-hour period, the following data were collected:

User number	Arrived at	Duration of use
1	09.30	2 minutes
2	09.40	3 minutes
3	09.41	2 minutes
4	09.42	3 minutes
5	09.44	1 minute
6	09.45	3 minutes
7	09.46	4 minutes
8	09.47	1 minute
9	09.49	2 minutes
10	09.50	1 minute
11	09.55	2 minutes
12	10.00	1 minute

The information allows a graphical presentation to be made, showing the use of the photocopier and the way in which the queue builds and its length varies. Figure 22 illustrates this. A time line is first drawn, to give a scale for the events. Above this, a band, labelled 'photocopier use', enables the duration of each use to be blocked in, relative to the time line. 'Start of use' and 'finish of use' allow these events to be indicated and labelled with the user number. Above this, an 'arrival' line is drawn, on which the arrival of each user (again designated by user number) can be recorded relative to the time line. Below the arrival line the queue, represented by user numbers can be depicted.

From the graphical presentation it can be seen that the photocopier was unused for only eight minutes during the half-hour of the survey and that arrival times are, indeed, 'bunched' together, with low rates of arrival at the beginning and end of the period. The greatest queue length was four users and this occurred on four occasions, the longest waiting time for service being nine minutes, with either two or four minutes being the most common waiting period.

Armed with the information from the survey it is now possible for the analyst to model what might have happened had there been two photocopiers. The basic assumptions about queue discipline remain unchanged, that is 'first come, first served' and nobody abandons the queue, but an additional assumption has to be made: that a user will make use of the first available photocopier.

The diagram (Figure 23) is similar to the previous, with the addition of 'start of use', 'use' and 'finish of use' bands for the second photocopier.

The results show that the queue has been eliminated on all but two occasions and, even then, the user had to wait for only one minute. Clearly the rate of use of each photocopier will now be much lower and the costs of this additional provision will have to be balanced against the perceived benefits for the users.

Simulation can provide useful insights for management; it must be remembered, however, that the results still need interpretation and consideration: they will not *prove* that a particular course of action is necessarily right. Managerial judgement is needed before action is taken but analysis can reduce the risk of making an expensive error.

Some sophisticated attempts at modelling and simulation of elements of library and information services have been made. Buckland[20] presents an interesting set of approaches.

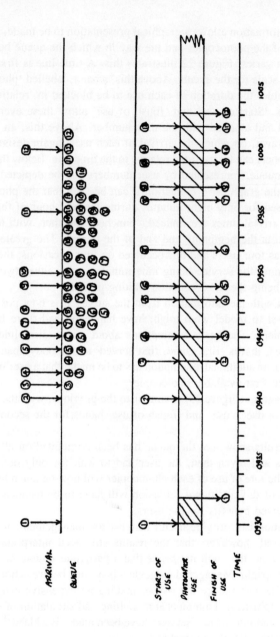

Figure 22 Simulation of system with one photocopier

118

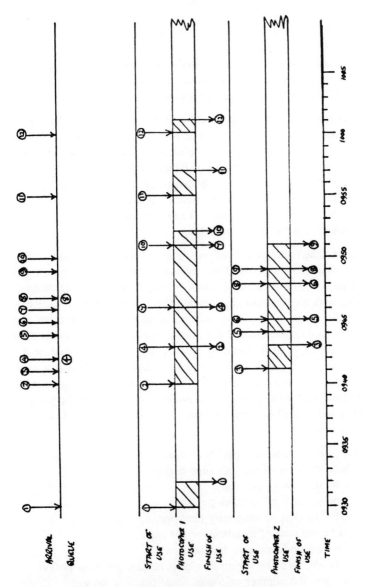

Figure 23   Simulation of system with two photocopiers

119

Cost models

Fundamental to most managerial decisions is an understanding of the way in which costs of the organization may be affected by a project. A cost model is a useful aid and can also provide a means of comparison between the old and the revised system and between one system and another.

The creation of a cost model depends on identifying the components of a process and then determining what each component costs. Each cost usually falls into one of three categories:

(a) *one-time costs* which represent payments incurred once. Examples are the purchase of equipment or costs for a staff training course;
(b) *fixed recurring costs* which represent fees or expenses incurred regularly but which do not vary. Examples are annual subscriptions for a service or a regular maintenance fee, costs of staff;
(c) *use-sensitive costs* which represent costs which vary in proportion to the activity of the system. Examples are costs of stationery, connect fees for online searching.

Consider the cost elements of providing a photocopier service, using a hired machine. The cost of hire of the equipment might be a fixed recurring cost (the duration of which will be the life of the agreement) together with a charge per copy made. This last will be a use-sensitive cost. Other use-sensitive costs will be supplies for the machine and electricity and maintenance if this is based on copy volume rather than the elapsing of fixed intervals of time. A one-time cost would be the production of a sign to advertise the service and explain how it is to be used. Some staff time would have to be spent each day in replenishing the machine and dealing with breakdowns: these costs could be grouped together and treated as fixed recurring costs. The cost model could be built up as follows:

Let C_T be the total cost per time period
   h be the cost of hire per time period
   c be the charge per copy
   s be the cost of supplies per copy
   e be the cost of electricity per copy
   m be the cost of maintenance per copy
   f be the one-time cost for the sign
   p be the fixed recurring cost of personnel per time period
   n equal the number of copies made per time period

For the first time period, the costs may be represented as:

$$C_T = h + n(c + s + e + m) + f + p$$

In successive time periods, the cost of the sign can be omitted because it is only a one-time cost. Alternatively, it could be shared over several successive time periods and treated as fixed costs but recurring only for a limited time.

The cost per copy made (C_C) in the first period can be expressed as:

$$C_C = c + s + e + m + \frac{(h + f + p)}{n}$$

The cost per copy will thus go down if more copies are made because the fixed and one-time costs are shared over a larger number of copies.

If charges for the use of the photocopier are to be made, the total revenue (T_R) from operations will vary with the price per copy (p) and the volume of copies:

$$T_R = n(p)$$

If full cost recovery is the aim then T_R must equal C_T, but the price at which this will occur will be unpredictable because the cost per copy will vary with the number of copies. Thus, it will be necessary for the management to take a view on what number of copies can be expected and whether to price to break even based on this number, to try to make a profit or to absorb a loss.

Costing is a complex topic and a full appreciation requires quite detailed study. Roberts[21] has written a thorough study of this matter.

Notes

1 Heather, P. and Stone, S., *CRUS guide 5: questionnaires*, Sheffield, Centre for Research on User Studies, University of Sheffield, 1984.

2 Line, M. B., *Library surveys: an introduction to the use, planning, procedure and presentation of surveys*, 2nd ed., revised by Sue Stone, London, Bingley, 1982.

3 Hoinville, G. Jowell, R. *et al.*, *Survey research practice*, Aldershot, Gower, 1985.

4 Jenkins, A. M. and Johnson, R. D., 'What the information analyst should know about body language', *Management information systems quarterly*, 1977, 33−48.

5 Belson, W. A., *Validity in survey research with special reference to the techniques of intensive interviewing and progressive modification for testing*

121

and constructing difficult or sensitive measures for use in survey research: a report, Aldershot, Gower, 1986.

6 Buzan, T., *Use your head*, London, BBC, 1974.

7 Stone, S., *CRUS guide 6: interviews*, Sheffield, Centre for Research on User Studies, University of Sheffield, 1984.

8 Moser, C. A. and Kalton, G., *Survey methods in social investigation*, London, Heinemann Education, 1971.

9 Mullings, C., *CRUS guide 7: observation*, Sheffield, Centre for Research on User Studies, University of Sheffield, 1984.

10 Stone, S. and Harris, C., *CRUS guide 1: designing a user study – general research design*, Sheffield, Centre for Research on User Studies, University of Sheffield, 1984.

11 Simpson, I. S., *Basic statistics for librarians*, 3rd ed., London, Bingley, 1988.

12 Swisher, R. and McClure, C. R., *Research for decision-making: methods for librarians*, Chicago, Illinois, American Library Association, 1984.

13 National Computing Centre, *Data processing documentation standards*, Manchester, NCC, 1977.

14 Daniels, A. and Yeates, D., *Basic systems analysis*, 3rd ed., London, Pitman, 1988, 30–52.

15 Veryard, R., *Pragmatic data analysis*, Oxford, Blackwell Scientific, 1984.

16 Rock-Evans, R., *Data analysis*, Sutton, IPC, 1981.

17 Avison, D. E., *Information systems development: a data base approach*, Oxford, Blackwell Scientific, 1985.

18 Bunday, B. D., *Basic queueing theory*, London, Edward Arnold, 1986.

19 Morse, P. M., *Library effectiveness: a systems approach*, Cambridge, Massachusetts, MIT, 1968.

20 Buckland, M., *Book availability and the library user*, Oxford, Pergamon, 1975.

21 Roberts, S. A., *Cost management for library and information services*, London, Butterworths, 1985.

5 *Systems design*

Introduction

The transition from analysis to design marks another of the points where the progress of the project ought to be reviewed. The feasibility study provides an opportunity to confirm or correct initial impressions and to make a decision to go ahead with further commitment of resources. After the analysis stage there is more information available about the nature of the system being investigated and a better assessment of needs of users and staff can be made. Some of the assumptions of the feasibility study may have been shown to be incorrect and other issues may have surfaced as a result of the investigation. A brief report by the analyst to senior management is desirable before major work on system design begins. It is also likely that the perception by management, staff and users of the desirable characteristics of any re-design will have changed as a result of the study so an opportunity to discuss such matters should be found. Once again, the key point is to build and reinforce a sense of commitment and involvement by all concerned with the new system.

The application of 'hard' methods of analysis, such as observation, flowcharting and structured interviews and 'soft' methods, such as group discussions, unstructured interviews and the production of 'rich pictures', will have created a body of data, some qualitative, some quantitative, which describes the existing system, identifies strong and weak points and indicates some useful lines of development. Much of this information might be called factual or objective, but it should be remembered that data collection always involves judgements about importance and salience: the decision about what is to be collected and the method of its collection will introduce a measure of subjectivity into the driest tabulation of figures. Some of the collected information will consist of opinion and explicitly subjective judgements, corroborated, perhaps, by similar expressions from other people. Some information will concern

123

hopes and aspirations for an improved service, or condemnation of especially bad aspects of the present service. The task of the system designer is to transform the analysis into a design for a new system which will meet the expectations of users and the performance standards defined by management. Thus, the final task of the analyst is to engender in management an understanding of the problems of the existing system and a commitment to the design of an improved system.

This may not be quite so easy as it might seem. Systems analysis, as a prelude to system design, is often started because senior management suspect there is an opportunity awaiting exploitation or some problem with the existing system which is causing it to perform at a less than acceptable level. Opinions as to the attractiveness of the opportunity or the cause of the problem may have been formed, positions established and sides taken. The analysis may have been undertaken almost as a last resort, in the hope that it will 'prove' someone right, or vindicate them. Very rarely is there no one with an axe to grind. The analyst, having had to make allowances for interpersonal behaviour during data collection, is now faced with similar problems of perception and organizational politics when presenting the results.

At the very least, it may be necessary to persuade management that their perception of the opportunity or problem is incorrect. The attractiveness of the opportunity or the magnitude and effects of the problem may have been over- or under-estimated, the problem may not be perceived as a problem by others. It is quite possible that the problem, as originally identified, is a symptom arising from some deeper malaise. Consider the following example.

An analyst from outside a library service was invited to comment on a problem. The service was a large, split-site library system. The original plan was for the analyst to assess the potential for automation of some of the activities of the library system. This involved an analysis of the work at the headquarters and outlying sites. Senior managers at headquarters were confident that automation was necessary. Their reason for this belief centred around the need to utilize resources effectively: they anticipated that an automated system could supply management information useful for the control of resources. In particular, they said, the outlying sites needed firmer direction from headquarters about resource utilization. The problem with the existing system was perceived as one of lack of control. It became clear that few of the staff at outlying sites were pleased that automation might be introduced and, whilst being fairly cooperative in supplying the information the analyst needed, it was

124

evident that the prospect of better resource control did not enthuse them. One day, whilst visiting one of the outlying sites, an informal discussion between the analyst and the site staff revealed strong feelings of antipathy towards the staff at headquarters. It was summarized well in the complaint: 'We've made many suggestions to headquarters about improvements to the service — but we get no answers.' Staff at other sites agreed strongly when this statement was put to them by the analyst, and they explained that it was simpler to introduce new ideas at a local level, rather than try to involve headquarters. The staff at the outlying sites were aggrieved at the lack of feedback from headquarters and were prepared to resist automation because it would tend to *enforce* more centralized control. 'Who will be in charge, then?' was the general cry.

The analyst, as consultant, saw that the task had been changed by these emerging feelings. It would be quite wrong to proceed with recommendation for automation without dealing with this major issue of staff attitudes. It had become necessary to demonstrate to senior management at headquarters that their perception of the problem in the system was only partly correct: in addition to whatever problems of control there might be, there was a much larger problem of ineffective communication and lack of feedback. To have proceeded with the design of a new system without having tackled this misperception would have been foolish. Whilst it is likely that the new system would have worked, after a fashion, it is apparent that its introduction would have been far from smooth and its use less than effective. Fortunately, the senior management were very receptive to the criticism that had been made and they acknowledged that pressure of work had often diverted their attention from assessing some of the ideas that had been offered. Further discussion revealed that the management of time was a significant problem for senior staff at headquarters and that much effort was being devoted to 'fire-fighting' and reactive management. So, in addition to the design of an automated system, a series of day-schools on time management was presented and staff from outlying sites and headquarters were invited. The first day-school centred on the identification of why time was sometimes wasted or effort diverted. This provided a useful forum for those from the outlying sites to develop their point about lack of feedback and poor communication. Because senior staff were already aware that this constituted a significant area of ill-feeling and because they had, privately, acknowledged that there was a problem, their response was not defensive except when they believed that a particular complaint was unjustified. This 'clearing of the air' resulted in the

125

discharge of much of the resentment felt by staff from the outlying sites and gave them some perception of the problems faced by senior staff at headquarters. Together they were able to work out a more satisfactory way of presenting and evaluating new ideas. The remainder of the day-schools concentrated on exploring techniques for improved time-management. The overall result was the establishment of a much more receptive atmosphere for the development of the automated system and, in particular, the acceptance by the staff of the outlying sites of the need for improved coordination of the use of resources.

This point in the system life cycle thus represents a critical stage in the development of an effective system. It is important that the findings of the analysis be fully discussed and that participants, at all levels in the organization, have an opportunity to comment, correct, ask questions and reveal doubts. The facilitation of this is an important task for the analyst, and group discussions should, wherever possible, be used. The amount of time, and the number and level of staff involved, will depend on the scale and likely effect of the problem or opportunity: a major redesign might involve meetings with most personnel, but the choice of a new photocopier might only involve personnel in a particular department. The principal objective is to arrive at an agreement about the nature of the opportunity or problem and whether it is still considered feasible to do anything about it. Clearly, this involves a judgement similar to that taken at the feasibility study stage, with the difference that there is better understanding about the nature of the commitment of resources which will be involved. Even at this stage, it is quite possible that the response will be that the gain from solving a problem or making use of an opportunity is too small or too uncertain compared with the anticipated level of resource utilization. Another response might be to shelve a project for the time being because its pursuance would divert resources from another project with greater, or less uncertain, benefits. Whatever the decision, whether it be to abandon, defer or to proceed, it should be clear and the reasons for the decision should be understood. It is unlikely, given human nature, that everyone will agree with the decision, but there is less chance of disagreement and the development of factions and organizational politicking if matters have been clearly resolved.

The desirability of agreement is evident if one considers the nature of the organizational climate during a period of change. Implicit in the view of change developed so far in this book is the recognition that change, as a *process*, is a necessary part of life, something to be

126

welcomed as evidence of vitality rather than shunned as a threat. Having become accustomed to thinking in terms of 'open systems', it is quite easy to accept the concept of change as being a way of life. Considerable quantities of organizational energy can be liberated during a period of change, and the careful manager will wish to channel such energy into productive purposes. It can easily be dissipated in arguments which lead to no satisfactory conclusion. The analyst facilitates the exchange of information, views and opinions, but this should be regarded as a means to the end of creating better solutions.

Identifying the design path

Having gained agreement that it is feasible to proceed with the design phase, the next consideration is that of identifying the most desirable path to a solution. It is quite possible that the foregoing discussions may already have made that evident but, quite often, an agreement can be reached on the desirability of meeting some specified need, without a firm decision on the best way that this should be done, even after quite extensive analysis. The discerning manager should be suspicious of circumstances where only one solution is offered: this may conceal a host of ulterior motives and the attempted settlement of old scores.

The task of the analyst at the start of the design stage is to promote a consideration by management of the several means by which their objectives might be achieved and user needs satisfied. Some problems will be susceptible to a narrow range of solutions, but time should always be spent in defining even these. It may be possible to develop many potential solutions for a major problem or opportunity, so this part of the design phase should be carefully managed. There is a danger, however, of becoming locked into discussion and consideration to the extent that no development path is identified: the 'analysis − paralysis' syndrome is to be avoided, so clear criteria (for example, cost of solution, time taken to implement, availability of suitable staff) for evaluating each possibility should also be decided.

In what follows, general guidelines will be given but many of the examples will relate to the introduction of computers into libraries and information services. Implementation of computer systems is a frequent and important feature of development but the tenets of good system design practice should be apparent in any process of system design, regardless of the precise nature of the system.

A list[1] of decision variables which might be used by the analyst and management to develop solutions would include:

(a) location of system inputs, outputs and processing – for example, could online search services be provided at local service points rather than centrally?

(b) response rate of the processing – for example, could search requests be accumulated and online searches carried out in a batch, once a week?

(c) mode and medium of data input – for example, for online searching is it preferable to use a terminal which produces a printed record of the search rather than a visual display?

(d) style and medium of data output – for example, should the output from online searches be presented in an alphabetical sequence, sorted by name of author?

(e) style of the human-system boundary (sometimes called 'the human–system interface') – for example, should the intending reader be present with the searcher during an online search?

(f) level of data aggregation in the system – for example, what records, if any, about the effectiveness of online searching should be kept?

Technical objectives, arising from the type of technology envisaged, will also influence the identification, analysis and selection of possible solutions. An outline list of such objectives would include:

(g) flexibility and maintainability – both concern the need for and the ease of changing the system. Some capacity for expansion should be included in the design and provision made for maintenance. Designers of computer-assisted systems often aim for 'graceful degradation' in their designs: this means that if one part of the system fails, or is withdrawn for maintenance, it should not lead to overall system failure, but will probably result in the suspension of some facilities or a poorer performance overall;

(h) schedule and cost – the design of systems which will have a short life, have to be implemented quickly to cope with some emergency, or designed to a severe cost constraint, may have to include short cuts which would, in favourable circumstances, be considered unacceptable;

(i) efficiency – an optimized system is often working close to, or at the limit of, its capacity. Whilst this may offer the most effective use of present resources it is a design strategy which may provide an obstacle to expansion and render the system unable to absorb extra workloads for even a short time. This is no argument for a sloppy design but management must decide when something is 'good enough for its purpose';

(j) integration – the systems approach forces the designer to recognize that any system is itself a subsystem of some larger system and must be designed to fit in with the other subsystems. Inputs, their nature and timing, may have to be considered as fixed characteristics, whilst outputs may have to be designed to fit in with the needs of other subsystems. In designing computer-assisted systems, several levels of integration are possible:

(i) the same data may be input to more than one subsystem (no integration);

(ii) printed output from one subsystem is entered by keyboarding into another subsystem (manual integration);

(iii) a file is output from one subsystem, recorded on magnetic tape and used as input to another subsystem (tape file integration);

(iv) a master file held on disc is updated by one subsystem and is available for access by another subsystem (disc master file integration);

(v) files are held in a database, accessible and modifiable by most subsystems (module-level integration).

(k) security – the design of secure systems involves both control on access and use of facilities and physical security. Adequate control should be built into the system as the design progresses because it is usually expensive to add such features to an established system. The need for control is not confined to aspects like the storage of security-classified data: audit requirements may necessitate the inclusion of tamper-proof audit trails (to provide a complete record of expenditure) and the ability to alter or delete the contents of files such as the main catalogue should be restricted. The need for physical security may necessitate the copying of important documents and files (such as the catalogue) and their secure storage away from the site;

(l) reliability – this includes accuracy of stored data, ability to recover from system failure or errors, reliability of equipment, instructions and, in a computer-assisted system, software. The design of highly reliable systems generally raises costs, so some managerial assessment of costs and resultant benefits from the increased reliability is needed. Even extensive duplication of equipment will be insufficient to ensure uninterrupted service availability (there is a small probability that 'back-up' facilities will also break down),

129

so system design should include the design of procedures for coping with system failure. The general design philosophy should be to facilitate easy testing of equipment and procedures, both on first development and at subsequent intervals to allow for maintenance. Unnecessarily complex designs may militate against this;

(m) portability − machinery (especially that using electronics) often has a design life of as little as five years. Other parts of a system, such as the general outline of procedures, can endure much longer and the manager may be faced with the task of replacing worn-out equipment without altering the essential processes which it supports. It is exceedingly difficult (if not impossible) to ensure that a system designed now will still be workable using equipment to be available five, ten, or more years hence. It is possible to reduce the difficulty by ensuring that the design does not include features which are essential but which depend for their working on facilities which are specific to one type of machine, machinery available from one manufacturer, or, in a computing environment, one type of programming language. Producers of computers often speak in terms of 'compatibility': that is, the ability to match the characteristics of one type of machine with another so that the machines may work together. Two orders of compatibility are commonly defined:

  (i) upward compatibility − procedures which work on one model in a range of computing equipment should also work on the more advanced models in the same range. This offers a development path as the workload on a system increases;

  (ii) forward compatibility − new equipment designs should still permit the use of facilities available on older equipment. This provides a development path as the demand for additional facilities increases.

In practice, it is not possible to guarantee complete portability and compatibility: the nature of a competitive market, coupled with rapid technological change, makes their pursuit something of an illusion. When portability is especially important, the system design should be simple, particularly in regard to the use of files and storage strategies, and should use a standard version of a programming language rather than a dialect of it;

(n) simplicity − simple solutions often provide the most effective answers: complexity may have more to do with the need to gratify the egos of designers and managers than satisfaction of user needs.

130

These should be considered in relation to the user needs already defined by the systems analysis and the resources available to satisfy them. The questions are designed to force decisions about the required levels of performance which the new system must attain in meeting user needs. The outcome of these considerations should be a firm commitment to a solution path which gives clear guidelines about expected facilities and performance. In dealing with a complex system, it may be useful to specify both mandatory requirements and additional 'nice-to-have' features. The first group will represent the necessary minimum design to meet needs and will control the design, whilst elements from the second can be included in the design as time and resources permit.

The process of system design

The process of designing a new or replacement system can be conveniently split into two parts: the development of a logical system and the development of a physical system capable of carrying out the logical activities. This strategy of separation provides a convenient period during which problems which may be revealed during design can be discussed with management before consideration is given to choice of equipment or particular forms of procedure. Another reason for the separation is to provide assurance that the system which is eventually implemented will have evolved from the needs of users. This point needs emphasis: it is all too easy for the designer and management to be carried along a particular route because the product of a particular manufacturer has captured their attention. The product may well appear to satisfy all the defined needs of the users and may offer other interesting features too. It may already have been installed at other sites having similar characteristics or have been demonstrated to admiring audiences at a conference. None of these is a sufficient reason for its purchase. Only when it has been evaluated against a profile of the requirements of a library or information centre can a reasonable decision be made. Part of the profile of requirements will have emerged as an aspect of the systems analysis, but the logical design stage will define further requirements. There is a cautionary tale from the early history of computer applications in business. An insurance company was encountering problems in linking names of policy holders with policy numbers. A senior manager had been to a conference at which products of the embryo computer industry were discussed. Salesmen from various companies were invited to give presentations about their company products. The Board of Directors was enthusiastic, especially about the power and speed of the machines. The Finance Director was rather cautious, especially when prices of several million pounds were mentioned: the Director suggested asking a consultant to review the problem and the proposed solutions. The consultant recommended the purchase of a set of index cards and the setting-up of a simple indexing system. One could, of course, argue that the company would eventually have benefited from the power of the computer system to carry out many other jobs, but this is to ignore the point: the effects of the problem as specified could be ameliorated quite simply and at low cost. If there is an expectation of other problems or the desire to take other opportunities, then these should be defined and carefully studied, rather than hoping that their solution will emerge as an unspecified by-product.

The degree of separation of the logical and physical design stages will depend upon the scale and nature of the project. A project to re-arrange staff responsibilities in a library or information service is unlikely to involve much in the way of technology or new equipment. Most of the design work will be logical: assigning duties to meet user needs, recognizing and defining training needs and developing a timetable for the changes. Little physical design will be involved, except, perhaps, adjustments to staff instructions, timetable schedules and so on. The design of a large sophisticated automated library processing system will entail considerable work on both the logical and the physical stages. The requirements of the users will usually be represented in terms of inputs and desired outputs from the system: for example, one might wish to input elements forming a bibliographic record and then use those elements in particular combinations and arrangements to produce catalogue records, orders for suppliers, circulation records and accessions listings. The design of the logical system entails the development of a network of steps by which the inputs are transformed into the desired outputs. User needs also define how the inputs and outputs are to be presented: in printed form, held in storage in a file, input or output when needed on a visual display unit and so on. The physical design stage will concentrate on how the inputs and outputs are to be made: what types of equipment will be needed, how fast their speed of processing should be, what storage capacity they should have. The physical system design will also include the specification and design of documentation and, for an automated system, the specification of computer programs. This last aspect is not to be confused with the writing of computer programs: rather, it is a description which the programmer can then use to develop a suitable program.

Organizing the design process

The importance of the logical design stage is evident, and it may be thought wise to continue the systematic approach already adopted in the analysis stages and look for an appropriate methodology which focuses attention and reduces the possibilities of omitting important details. A useful approach, adopted by IBM in the 1960s, is the *study organization plan*, often abbreviated to SOP. It was originally intended for use in developing computer-assisted management information systems, but there is no reason why the approach should not also be applied to the design of manual systems or the design of simple computer-assisted systems.

The core of the study organization plan is the specification of the new system in terms of inputs and outputs, files, operations, activities and resource usage (see Figure 24). For each separate activity, an operation sheet, message and file sheet, are developed and the appropriate resource needs listed on the resource usage sheet. Next, for each activity, a measure of efficiency is defined by which a manager could judge whether the system is performing adequately. For example, if the activity is the recording of loans in a circulation control system, the analysis phase should have provided evidence of the pattern of demand for this service.

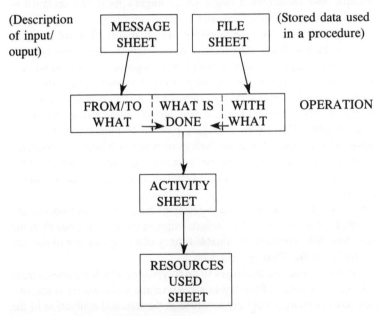

Figure 24   Study organization plan

133

This pattern will suggest what transaction rates must be accommodated if queues are to be kept down to a length considered acceptable. The key point is that the synthesis of operation description, time taken to carry out an operation and a managerial view on aspects of service management, such as queueing, provide clear guidelines on desired performance and a means of choosing between different types of equipment, different configurations and methods of working.

The logical design process is a necessary first step towards developing a system specification which will provide potential suppliers with information about the precise requirements to be satisfied by the new system. As with the preceding stages of the system life cycle, every effort should be made to involve the users or potential users in the design process through consultation and discussion. In this way the implications of choices and compromises made during the design process can be evaluated, inadequacies and incorrect assumptions revealed, and suitable corrections made before commitment to a particular design is made.

Many users, including senior management, may find it quite difficult to visualize the system if presented with only the logical design: it takes a leap in the imagination to transform a flowchart description, for example, into the screen dialogue which might appear on a terminal as part of an acquisitions system and a still greater leap to imagine what working with that dialogue might be like. It is often helpful to try to simulate the working of the proposed new system through 'prototyping'.

In essence, a prototype is a model of a proposed system, subsystem or process. It does not have to be real but it should be realistic: it is an aid to thinking and assessing reactions so it should give participants an opportunity to explore how the development might change the nature of their jobs. The screen dialogue, previously mentioned, could be presented as a series of 'frames' written on paper or it might be simulated on a terminal. It would not be necessary to have a full working acquisitions system if the aim is to facilitate an evaluation of the screen dialogue.

As a result of comments and suggestions made during evaluation, the prototype may be changed to include improvements. The growth of the prototype thus represents a valuable history of a project and will provide the basis for the final specification.

There are some disadvantages to prototyping of which the design team will need to be aware. Prototyping takes time and will consume resources, especially if many people are involved in the trial and evaluation of the prototypes. On the other hand, it can be argued that the selection and enforcement of an inappropriate design on an unwilling user group will lead to dissatisfaction and decline in efficiency. The basis for comments of participants in the evaluation process will tend to be their individual and collective experience of the old system and there may be a reluctance to think beyond its confines. Another possible disadvantage is that several conflicting views may emerge rather than a consensus. Vested interests may seek to use such differences of opinion to slow down or halt the development of the new system; the conservatism inherent in many groups may seek to return to the old system or to include all the features of the old system in the design for the new.

There are no easy answers to these problems. At the outset, it is best to recognize that prototyping of every aspect of a new system may be very expensive and that it is probably unnecessary in circumstances where there are few alternative ways of doing something. If there is already a good example, which has been found by others to be quite workable in similar conditions, its use should be considered. Prototyping is best reserved for design areas where there is no robust paradigm and where there are stakeholder groups which might have a strong and legitimate interest in them. Vested interests are best dealt with by encouraging their open expression; this can often be achieved during a discussion of the design problems surrounding the prototype under review by seeking agreement on a range of criteria which will be used to judge aspects of the design. By shifting the focus for discontent from the prototype to the criteria for its evaluation it should be possible to air the disagreements, find common ground and then use agreed criteria for a rather more dispassionate review of the prototype. The prototype is thus acting as a mediator between the concerns of the various groups and the final design. Demand is driving design, which is as it should be.

The role of management must not be forgotten. It is the right and the responsibility of managers to manage and the use of a participative approach to design evaluation does not reduce this responsibility. Advice, opinion and conjecture have to be translated into a decision and this is a proper role for management. However committed a manager may be to a participative approach to design there is a point at which discussion and the comparison of designs must stop and a choice must be made. The ideal would be for this transition to occur quite naturally: a consensus would become apparent after a short time of discussion and comparison and this would be recognized by the group, accepted as being the best choice and implemented by management. The problem arises when discussion does not lead to such consensus, appears to be indeterminate

135

or when management cannot accept the recommendations.

Handling such events can call for tact and firmness. If a culture of participation has been established then the sudden transition, or reversion, to decision-making by senior management will be resented even if it cannot be resisted. Any trust which has been built up may quickly be replaced by cynicism and later attempts at participation will be much harder to establish. A better understanding of this behavioural problem can be found if the expectations of the stakeholders in the discussion group are considered. The manager is aware of the need to arrive at a solution which can operate within certain resource constraints; in addition, the manager is aware of the need to meet deadlines so that the process of design is not impeded. The objective of the manager is to seek agreement, within a certain time, on a solution which meets certain criteria. Other group members will bring an assortment of opinions and attitudes but they will not be aware of the pressures on the manager unless these are openly acknowledged and discussed. A participative approach to design can only be successful if all participants are aware of the true objectives of the meeting and the criteria for selecting a solution. At the outset, the manager should outline the timetable and constraints and then encourage a discussion of the features and facilities which should be represented in an acceptable design. This should encourage all participants to take part in creating the agenda, thus involving themselves in the management of the discussion. The group adopts and assumes responsibility for operating within the constraints outlined by the manager rather than being told that it must conform. At the outset, the manager should promote a consideration of how to bring discussions to a conclusion: voting is unlikely to be a suitable method because it splits groups into 'winners' and 'losers' and leaves fertile ground for the seeds of argument to sprout if problems with the design should later emerge. It is better to seek a method with some semblance of objectivity such as ranking, where the relative position in the rank of each design can be debated and participants will have an opportunity to modify their views. At the same time, the group must recognize that if no agreement is possible the responsibility, and the right, of choice rests with the manager.

Participation is a method of management which needs careful handling and the development of a supportive culture if it is to be successful and satisfying for both the manager and the participants. It is essential for the manager to consider how well it might fit in with the history and prevailing culture of the organization. It will not be successful if introduced suddenly into an organization where the management style has been largely authoritarian. It will not suit circumstances where a manager has already, mentally, made a choice and is seeking support. It will not be acceptable if there is really no effective choice to be made, where there is no viable alternative. Participation depends on all members being ready to listen to each other and willing to work towards a solution. Trust is essential and cannot be built up immediately.

Users and system design

Most library and information systems, whether they are manual or make use of computers, involve the creation and use of records and files. Data are collected, input to the system, processed in some way and data may then be output. As far as the user is concerned, the input and the output represent the system: attitudes to the system are formed largely by experience of inputting data and receiving output. The processing of the data, its storage and retrieval, transmission, copying and verification are aspects which are largely hidden and of no direct interest to most users, except insofar as these activities may affect the input to, and output from, the system. For this reason, the design of the input and output routines should be given particular attention. In many cases, the design of the input and output routines is the point at which the knowledge and insight of the professional librarian or information worker can be most usefully linked to the skills of other professionals, such as computer programmers or systems engineers, who may be responsible for the design of the processing and other 'hidden' routines which form the core, as distinct from the periphery, of the system. The design of the core routines may need specialized knowledge or skills or, in contrast, may be designed according to a standard set of procedures. The point is that the library or information service, as a client, may not be *able* to have much influence on this part of the design because it uses a corpus of knowledge from outside the professional domain of the library or information worker and thus constitutes a 'black box' as far as the remainder of the system is concerned: data is input, processed according to the rules established for the system and output is produced, but exactly how this is done may be a mystery to the client. The peripheral routines, on the other hand, form the link between the hidden core and the operating environment: they are tangible and need to respond to other components of the operating environment in an intelligent and helpful way.

For the remainder of this chapter, the model for a consideration of the design of input procedures, outputs and processes will be that of a computer-assisted system. Many of the general ideas and points made would, though, be applicable to manual systems.

This point about general applicability can be developed a little further: the argument throughout this book is that some general ideas of systems management are applicable to the problems encountered in running library and information services, just as they are applicable to the management of many other enterprises. Analysis, studies of feasibility, development and evaluation of different methods of solving problems or making use of opportunities: all have been found appropriate. Some techniques may work better on certain types of problem, so the manager is always concerned with choosing the most appropriate technique. In a study which resulted in the development of a contingency model of leadership, Fiedler and Chemers[2] suggested that a characteristic of a successful leader is the ability to use several leadership styles. We can now suggest that successful managers are those who are aware of many techniques for problem-solving or design and, whilst not necessarily being skilled in the use of them all, are able to draw their existence to the attention of those who could learn how. Such awareness often means being able to recognize that a technique from some other area of study could be of value in the manager's own area. The use of statistical techniques is a good example.

In relation to designing, providing and managing information services, the computer industry has proved useful by encouraging designers to consider very carefully the job of collecting and inputting information and the form of the output. This is because it is, at present, difficult to design computing systems which are as tolerant of errors, inconsistencies and special cases as human beings. Consider, for example, a form to apply for membership of some club or social organization. One is faced, perhaps, with the impossible task of squeezing full name, in block capitals into an inadequate space. Most people try, perhaps allowing their names to spill over into the margin or on to the next line. It doesn't matter too much, because the input system and the processing system (human beings, paper and pens) are flexible enough to cope. But, what happens if the paper application form is replaced with a computer terminal? Now the human being is faced with something which is fairly inflexible. If the system designer has anticipated dealing with names of up to twenty characters only, then no amount of special pleading on the part of the hapless human will persuade the system to accept a name longer than this. The problem can occur at the output stage, too, as a library found to its cost some years ago. The installation of a new

138

circulation control system necessitated the printing of computer-readable readers tickets. Each ticket carried the name of the reader: first forename, followed by surname. To save on production costs, the system designers had decided to print only the first six letters of the forename. The librarians were somewhat unprepared for the influx of complaints from the many Christophers, Christines and Christabels, but these paled into insignificance compared to a forthright gentleman called Brendan.

An example of a different kind is offered by the automatic cash dispensers at some bank branches. When these first appeared, the messages which were displayed after one's card had been accepted prompted the customer to input on the keyboard the sum of money required in multiples of £5. Groups of puzzled people could be seen to gather as they weighed up whether to type in say, '3' if they wanted £15, or to type in '15'. The designer of the system knew exactly what was meant by that message, but intending customers were faced with an ambiguity. Fortunately, most people did discover fairly quickly what was the expected response; the message has, in any case, now been changed.

All of this points to the need to design input and output routines for systems using computers with care, but it is clear that what has been painfully learnt in the developing information technology industry may also be applicable to manual systems. Examine the range of forms which users are expected to complete to use library and information services, the instructions they are asked to obey and explanations which they are offered: are they really good enough? Are they clear and unambiguous, suitable for their purpose, up-to-date and easy to use? Do they ask for information which is no longer relevant? For many users or potential users, the first impression of a service is gained from having to cope with such materials. Good graphic design and quality printing count for something, but even simple forms or notices produced with typewriter and photocopier should be carefully planned. Above all, a design should be tested, ideally by asking someone outside the project team to fill in the form or read the notice or try to obey the instructions. It is usually an instructive exercise, provided one does not dismiss its findings or draw comfort from the assumption that there will always be someone around to explain things and so it is not really worth altering the design.

It is good practice to use prototypes as a means of gathering reactions to forms, sequences of instructions and outputs from systems, regardless of whether use is made of computers or not. Much useful information can be gained from such exercises, especially if a small group of the intended users of the forms, instructions and so on can be included.

It is also necessary to consider how the system is to prompt the user to supply information, what should happen if incorrect or invalid information is entered and what should happen if the user does not know what to do. It is worth remembering that systems which are likely to be used by 'the public' should be robust and capable of offering assistance and explanations in circumstances when it may be far from clear what the user wants to do. A casual look round the public areas of a library or some little experience of working at an enquiry counter will convince most professional librarians and information workers that, if computer-assisted systems are offered, they will be tested, perhaps to destruction, by the users. A consideration of the range of enquiries, the many and various ways of posing those enquiries and the range of responses to the answers provided by a professional service must prompt questions about whether any automated system can cope. The success of bank cash dispensers must, in part, be attributable to the limited range of tasks expected of them, but it is the clear definition and the low level of ambiguity of those tasks which allows their successful automation. Even so, there can be problems over lack of familiarity: the story of the man driving into a self-service petrol station, stuffing a five pound note up the spout of the petrol pump and shouting 'Two gallons, please' may be apocryphal, but it illustrates the extreme difficulty of designing automated systems which will cope under all conditions.

The lesson which is being slowly learnt is probably very common. In the early days of technical developments, useful technical progress is probably hampered as much by enthusiasts as by those who oppose. The enthusiast sees the development in universal terms: something which will transform life and free us from this or that ill. No sane person would be without its benefits. The opposition sees the development as threatening to life: no sane person would think of adopting or supporting it. As the dust settles a little, experience begins to suggest for what purpose the development might actually be useful. Finally, it becomes accepted as a tool to assist, alongside a range of other tools. The proper task for the manager then becomes the selection of the most appropriate tool for the job at hand. An example from an analogous field may help: consider the clamour surrounding the commercial development of microfilm systems in the 1960s. These were, it was said, about to transform libraries and even personal collections. 'The book is dying!' said the Cassandras. The revolution has taken somewhat longer than promised and has taken a quite different route. Microfilming has been found to be very suitable for a small range of jobs: it has its good points and its weaknesses.

So, the astute manager is always sceptical and there is nothing about the development of automated systems which should persuade the manager to make an exception. Automation and the use of computers may have an impact on rather more of life than the development of other tools, but the principle should remain the same: there will be some activities for which the computer is admirably suited, some for which it offers no particular advantages over other methods, and some for which it is quite unsuitable. It may be wondered, for example, whether the development of some OPACs is an entirely unmixed blessing. Some systems appear to be very easy to use, tolerant and able to offer useful suggestions if the user is puzzled about how to proceed. Other systems, though, appear to be slightly modified versions of systems intended, essentially, for the use of cataloguing staff. They are intolerant and do not offer helpful, or comprehensible, messages when errors occur. No doubt such systems could be redesigned to overcome these problems, but what is the motive of library and information service managers for offering these to the public in their crude form? Is it to impress users and policy-makers that the service is modern and worth funding? Is it to impress other managers that this library service *is* progressive? Is it to try to provide a level of assistance to users that cannot be provided by other means? All of these, and more, might be advanced as reasonable, or partly reasonable, justifications. The provision of such unsatisfactory systems must prompt a question as to whether a greater awareness of user need, patterns of searching and expectations should be gained before exposing users to raw technology. This is not to suggest that experiments should not be carried out: such work is needed if greater understanding is to be gained, but the essence of experimentation is control and observation. The design of responsive automated systems which combine error control, generous guiding and useful results from a variety of input data and for a variety of purposes is a current problem and it may be that a realistic managerial judgement is to concentrate, at present, on raising standards of personal assistance by providing automated systems for staff use rather than expecting clients to cope with the malevolent glow of unforgiving visual display unit terminals.

Input design: checklist[3] of convenient features

Whether a system is easy and convenient to use can make the difference between success and failure. It can also make the difference between a system which is well liked and used often, and one which is avoided, resented and misused. Good input (and output) design is concerned with providing features which match naturally the pace, sequence and demands of a job, which tolerate mistakes or forgetfulness, which aid new users, but do not get in the way of skilled workers, and which produce responses that make sense.

A cardinal principle should be to avoid requiring the user to enter information which the system can supply of its own accord (for example, the current date) or from previously supplied information (for example, the address of a library supplier where a list of the names and addresses of suppliers is already stored as a file elsewhere in the system). This principle is also linked with the idea of providing 'default' values for some inputs. This means that system is designed to suggest values which the user can reject and change or accept by not changing them (that is, 'by default'). This is further considered below.

Another cardinal principle is to design systems where data is input once and is used to build a complete record. A good example is the progressive addition of information to a bibliographic record as a document moves from the stage of being ordered (fairly scant information, sufficient for the supplier to identify the required item, being needed), through accessioning and cataloguing. Integrated systems may provide further facilities by allowing much of the data to be compiled from other sources such as cooperative databases: the necessary input then becomes that of control information (to identify the required data) and local information (such as accession numbers, location and numbers of copies) for administrative purposes.

In addition, well-designed input systems should:

(a) provide default values for inputs where the information is likely to be repetitive (for example, in a cataloguing system, the year of publication, if most of the documents acquired are current publications). The system should display such default values and give the user the option of accepting or changing them;

(b) prompt the user to input data, but allow skilled users to work with a shorter sequence of prompts (or,even, no prompts at all) than novices. 'Help pages' should be provided which can be summoned at any point during data input, read and acted upon without affecting the data already input. The text needs to be carefully written and reviewed to ensure it is relevant and helpful, but should refrain from offering long explanations or lists of alternatives: if this is unavoidable they should be provided in a manual, the 'help page' serving to draw attention to the appropriate part of the manual;

(c) scan all input data to ensure that it matches the form, type and range of data expected (for example, numerals might be expected in a date field; prices for single copies of current publications might normally not be expected to exceed £150). Some input data may already include means of checking for validity (for example, the 'check digit' of an International Standard Book Number): the system should be designed to make use of this. If the input fails to match, the system should provide an informative error message which shows why the input has been queried, an example of acceptable input, and the means of correcting the data. In some circumstances, data which does not pass the matching check may still be valid: the system, having drawn attention to the possible error, should provide means of making a correction or of confirming that the data is correct.

The design of procedures for checking data is a complex and interesting topic. As more processes are designed to be controlled using computers, so the need to develop better means of data validation will also grow. In relation to input design, the manager of a library or information service needs to ask what effect the input of invalid data may have on the integrity and effectiveness of the information service. Some errors are bound to creep in, some may be very expensive to exclude. The manager has to make some judgement about the risk compared with the cost of screening.

Data input by staff in libraries and information services is usually concerned with the addition, deletion or amendment of records in fields or databases, that is, the keyboarding of data to build up or maintain records. In most cases, data input is a costly and labour intensive process. Although research is being carried out into alternative methods of data input, such as direct optical recognition of printed or handwritten characters by computers, it is fair to say that the commercial exploitation of such systems in libraries and information services lies somewhat in the future. The use of optical recognition of bar-codes and mark-sensing as methods of inputting data for circulation control is a useful technique, but depends for its success on the limited amount of data that has to be input for each record. For example, the bar-coded label used by many libraries records a 10-digit accession number in a space of 55 millimetres. Just imagine the length of a bar-code to record even a fairly simple author and title statement. It seems likely that keyboards will be in use for some time to come and thus the need to design the flow of work at the input

143

stage will remain of importance if speedy and accurate working is to be achieved.

Output design: checklist[4] of convenient features

Consistency and utility are the cardinal principles. The choice of a suitable *form* of output is linked to anticipated use. Great care should be exercised when designing any form of output, but especial attention should be given to output which is likely to be sent to, or used, by clients or customers. Whilst staff should not be expected to cope with inadequate or ill-designed output, they may be expected to tolerate the presentation of frequently used data in a coded or compressed form. Clients are unlikely to be willing to invest the effort into decoding unless the information is vital. Is it clear, for example, that '32 p.' in a bibliographic record refers to the number of pages rather than the price?

In particular, well-designed systems should:

(a) provide outputs, displays and reports which are consistent with the needs of a particular process (for example, are the full names of authors needed in both the catalogue record and the records for the accounting procedures?). Wherever possible, a consistent style of presentation is to be desired, but slavish adherence to it may not be helpful;

(b) give the user the ability to control the quantity and extent of output (for example, it should be possible to specify output of only the most recent records, and to restrict the output to desired parts of each record), but provide a default format and quantity. It should also be possible to interrupt the output if irrelevant material has, by mistake, been selected. The remorseless generation of screens of information or yards of paper printout is irritating, especially if the user is not yet convinced that the data will prove useful. Before outputting, the system should warn the user of the anticipated volume which will be produced, if it exceeds a threshold value (e.g. 10 printed pages), and ask for confirmation that the user wishes the system to proceed;

(c) use typographic and graphic means of drawing attention to significant features in the output (for example, records to be checked by cataloguing staff might have suspect data underlined);

(d) provide output in physical forms suitable for intended use. Printed output may be required for some processes (for example, book orders to be despatched to suppliers); careful choice of layout and headings

144

and, perhaps, printed stationery, will greatly facilitate its use. Some care should be taken to select a printing technique which produces copy acceptable to the user, but is economical in use and reasonably fast to produce. If possible, the system should offer alternative output forms: for example, it might be convenient to search the catalogue from a visual display unit terminal, and then be able to print out details of items judged to be relevant.

Output design is influenced strongly by the use to which the output data are to be put. Managers, for example, may well be able to define their need for control information, but may find it convenient for that information to be presented in the form of graphs or tables. Users of an information retrieval system may favour systems which highlight the terms from their search statement which have been matched in each retrieved record. As personal experience of using computer-assisted systems increases, so does the desire to link data derived from one process with another. For example, an obvious question arising from a search in an information retrieval system is: 'Are these items available here, and now?' This implies the need for a link with other parts of a system, allowing queries to be passed to the circulation control system and for this to be possible without the tedious typing of information already discovered. Thus, a consideration of the characteristics of output, combined with some study of how users might be expected to make use it, may lead a designer to refine the design of the associated process and to consider accommodating linkages with other parts of the system.

Process design
Despite the point made in an earlier section about the limited effect that library or information service personnel may have upon the design of processes in computer-assisted systems, it is worth identifying those areas where some influence can have effect. These relate, as might be expected, to points where the characteristics of the core of the system have a strong effect on the periphery.

The goal of many system designers has been the development of integrated systems: that is, systems which offer a complete suite of programs capable of exchanging data and allowing the user to pass from using one part of the system to another without difficulty. Progress on providing integrated systems for libraries and information services has been slow, partly because the provision of computing resources has not been adequate to support such approaches, partly because development costs for in-house systems have been high and partly because the market for such systems has not been perceived to be great enough by potential manufacturers. The growth in the cooperative provision of computing resources for libraries and information services has now made the development of integrated systems a more practical proposition, both because powerful machines can be provided and because it is possible to employ staff who can concentrate on the analysis and design of procedures suitable for the cooperating libraries. It is not often acknowledged that the move towards joining cooperatives also represents a willingness to accept a certain amount of standardization. Designing and running, for example, five entirely separate and distinct cataloguing systems for five libraries is of dubious economy. A better proposition is to design one system which forms a common core of processes accepted by the five and then 'tailor' the input and output aspects of the system to suit the special needs of each library. Even here, the process designer will probably seek some standardization: the manager of the library service has to be clear as to what features of the existing system are essential for the satisfactory functioning of the whole organization and which must be preserved, or provided in some other way, in the new design.

The manager may also need to guide the system designer as to the desired currency of the files maintained by the processes. For example, in designing the order process for an acquisitions system, some consideration must be given to the job of updating the order file as new orders are input. Should such orders be added immediately to the order file? To use the jargon, should the order file be updated in real time? Such an approach will mean that any enquiries made of the order file will always retrieve an up-to-date picture of the state of the file. The alternative would be to design the process so that new orders, and alterations and amendments to existing orders, would be cumulated in a temporary transaction file which would then be used to update the main order file periodically. The main order file would be slightly out-of-date whenever enquiries were made, unless the enquiry happened to follow on immediately from the updating. Only the library or information service manager can decide whether the consequences of using such a method of 'batch' processing would offer a significant administrative problem, but the system designer would be able to advise on the relative design and running costs of each method and might be able to suggest other strategies such as developing a searching method which would automatically examine the contents of the main and the temporary files, thus concealing the mechanics of the system from the enquirer.

Speed of response is another characteristic which falls within the purview of the manager. One might suppose that immediate response to enquiries made of a system is always a desirable and necessary characteristic. It may be inhibiting, however, if the response is so quick that it startles the enquirer. On the other hand it is well-known that responses which, at first, seemed very fast can appear to become very tardy as familiarity with the system develops. The speed may be the same, but it is the perception of it that has changed. Speed will also be affected by system loading: just as delays in being served may be experienced at busy times in shops, so a heavily loaded computer system will offer a slower response. The managerial decision is concerned with how long a delay it is reasonable to tolerate, and at what cost, compared with the cost of providing extra computer resources to lessen such delays.

Another aspect of response time is whether it is always necessary for the system to produce answers to enquiries immediately. For example, in requesting a report on issue statistics, is it reasonable to expect a manager to wait one hour for its production? What about a delay of one day? By contrast, what about a financial report? Managerial judgements about the acceptability of these response times are governed by the urgency of the matter which prompts the enquiry but the assessment should also include some consideration of the necessary speed with which decisions *have* to be made. There can be few managerial problems in the context of library and information work which require the same immediacy of response as, say, the management of money markets.

There are trade-offs to be made in system design between speed of processing and overall system costs. Fast speeds require powerful and expensive equipment used in the context of processes designed to facilitate such responses. In considering the design of a practical system, the manager should be encouraged to specify responses at speeds which are suitable and necessary for each area. Where experience suggests fast responses are needed, such as in responding to a catalogue enquiry or at the circulation control service point, provide them, but do not assume that all processes should necessarily be so responsive.

Security
There are trade-offs, too, in the matter of system security. It is unfortunate, but perhaps understandable, that the library and information science literature does not record many examples of disasters caused, or amplified, by failure of computer-assisted systems. Perhaps we have

147

been lucky: there are examples of companies which have ceased trading largely because the records vital to their business had been destroyed or become inaccessible through computer malfunction or operator error.

Specific areas to be considered are:

1   *Access*: although most libraries and many information services do not deal with material which is confidential or subject to high security classifications, certain parts of a computer-assisted system should have controls on access included in their design. Systems which store or offer access to security-classified material, proprietary information or other material to which access is to be limited, should incorporate procedures for checking attempts at making access. Many systems are designed around hierarchical file access structures (directories), which partition the database into successively more 'sensitive' levels. Access to higher levels may be controlled through the use of passwords or the use of terminals dedicated to this purpose and used under supervision. All attempts to use the system may also be 'logged' to ensure that attempts at illegitimate access are recorded. Legislation, notably the Data Protection Act 1984, insists on the control of access to files containing data describing clients of the service (for example, registration files and circulation records). The service is obliged to reveal to clients the fact that their names are recorded in such files and allow clients to see the information so recorded. The service must also demonstrate that access by people other than authorized staff could be prevented. It is very difficult to ensure that unauthorized access is not possible and it is, in the absence of case law, unclear exactly how this legislation will be interpreted.

2   *Financial control*: a means of checking financial procedures and accuracy of records will be insisted on by most organizations. Most will have an agreed set of control procedures which are to be built into the system design. Essentially, such procedures serve to create an 'audit trail' of records which are, supposedly, resistant to tampering and erasure. The records are then used by auditors to check that all expenditure is valid, correctly identified and recorded. The construction of audit trails is complex: a task best left to the financial experts.

3   *Data verification*: procedures for verification at the input stage are considered in an earlier section of this chapter. At the output stage it is useful for checks to be made to ensure that the output is within acceptable parameters. There are fewer reports now of bills for nil pounds and pence being sent to customers, largely due to system design features which 'trap' such oddities and alert the system operators to a likely

problem. Library and information service systems might include checks on the production of information sent to users: for example, would it make sense to send out a recall notice containing no information about the documents to be returned? Some fault in the processing might be indicated by such an error.

4 *File security*: some files may be designated as 'read only'. This designation would ensure that the user is prevented from adding to or altering the file contents. For example, it is essential to prevent catalogue users (other than cataloguers) from erasing catalogue entries! The alternative 'privilege' is 'read/write' (the user is able to both retrieve and amend data). The privileges may be associated with passwords, thus granting extra facilities if the correct code is first input.

5 *Back-up*: it is clearly important to ensure that both data files and program files can be reinstated in the event of loss or corruption by operator error or system fault of master files. Copies of data and program files can be made on to media such as magnetic tape or disc and then stored in safety, preferably away from the building containing the computer. Large (mainframe) computer systems often incorporate standard procedures to produce such security copies periodically, but the problem is much more acute with the proliferation of microcomputer systems where data and programs are often held on 'floppy' or 'hard' discs and where the system may not be under the supervision of a computing professional. It is human nature to put off the rather boring task of copying ('backing-up'), but bitter experience may teach one the need to do this job regularly. Outbreaks of computer 'viruses' which systematically destroy or corrupt data are a worrying phenomenon. The viruses are actually computer programs which have been illegally or inadvertently copied into a computer system, the intention of the program designer being to disable the host computer. The importation of the virus is often unnoticed until too late because it is buried in an otherwise legitimate program. Only when data starts disappearing does the presence of the virus become apparent and it is, by then, too late. If back-up copies of data and program files have not been kept then much damage to the system can occur.

6 *Physical security*: failure of the electricity supply is fairly uncommon in the UK, but mains fluctuation is not. Lightning strikes, flickering fluorescent lights, electric motors and other appliances may produce power surges which can cause computers to 'lock-up' and fail to respond. Large computer installations usually include devices to filter and smooth the mains supply; similar devices are available for

microcomputer installations. Large installations may also include independent power supplies for short-term use, to allow an orderly shutdown or maintenance of service at a reduced level, in the event of mains failure. Some manufacturers are producing protected power supply systems for use with microcomputers, but they are expensive.

Other aspects of physical security are concerned with preventing damage in the event of fire, flood or other calamity. Ensuring that data and program files are copied and stored away from the computer equipment (and heat, damp, dust and magnetic fields) is the most important point: computer equipment can be quickly replaced, but data may be irreplaceable.

The subject of security is often treated as being a highly technical matter. Certainly, the design of security procedures and the design of procedures to recover from points where that security has been compromised or after malfunction, are complex and need the expertise of the system designer. However, it is important that the manager has an underlying grasp of the need for, and effect of, such procedures. Only the manager can answer the question: 'What will be the effect on this organization of the failure of this system or the loss, corruption, or inadvertent publication, of that data?' Systems having a very high level of security will be expensive to design, run and maintain, because they are usually complex and incorporate lengthy checking procedures. Data may be stored several times on different storage media to provide paths for recovery if one set of data is destroyed. Some procedures, such as record deletion, may be accessible only after inputting passwords. Access to data of certain types may be similarly controlled. Only the manager can decide whether expenditure on the design of security features is justified, though it is clear that some security may be required by other interest groups for financial and audit purposes and to comply with legislation.

The system specification
The design of a successful system can be seen to be the product of collaboration: principally, the manager and the system designer have to work together to produce a workable, economic and effective design but users and constraints within the operating environment should have a shaping effect at various stages of the process. The special responsibility of the manager is to balance risk, facility provision and performance against development, running and maintenance cost. Some compromises will usually have to be made: the manager must know the needs,

priorities, expected performance and patterns of working of the library or information service if satisfactory decisions about the design are to be made.

The product of the exchange of ideas, discussion of compromises and exploration of alternatives will be a system specification. It is essential that the systems specification reflects accurately the needs of users and the constraints which have been identified because it will be used as the basis for seeking tenders from potential suppliers.

The specification is also a vital part of the management of the project. As well as recording needs and constraints it will identify important aspects such as means of control of input and output, security of data and the general plans for implementation. The specification must provide an outline, at a general level, of the complete system to be produced and then give a more detailed view, through the use of flowcharts and other descriptions, such that the purpose of the system and the means to achieve it should quickly become evident to the reader. It must also be easy to review the timetable and procedures for implementation, including the identification of any special problems or the need for particular kinds of equipment. Constraints, such as cost, time and use of staff, should also be recorded.

Each specification will be different because each refers to a specific system within a particular operating environment but a general outline of sections to include is:

(a) introduction — indicating the aim of the specification and the objectives of the project;

(b) general requirements — these are derived from the specific objectives identified for the system and will include factors such as a brief description of the operating environment for the system, identification of the intended user groups, an outline description of the system and an outline of the overall mandatory and desirable requirements;

(c) detailed requirements — for each identified subsystem or identifiable process there should be a statement of aims and objectives, general and particular requirements and detailed description. Particular points to consider for inclusion are security requirements, means for dealing with unusual circumstances and requirements for the provision of management information;

(d) general technical requirements — an outline of the required capabilities of the hardware and other machinery needed. In

151

particular, requirements as to reliability (remembering that all equipment will fail: the manager is concerned with specifying what frequency of failure can be tolerated), maintenance, provision of back-up in case of equipment failure, methods of installation, and perceived paths for development if the system is to be introduced as part of a progressive plan;

(e) detailed technical requirements — for each major component, such as hardware, software, data conversion and communications a detailed specification should be provided giving details of configuration, links with other system components, capacity, speed of response, reliability, and error detection and correction, as appropriate;

(f) validation criteria — a specification of expected performance, including tests the components must be able to pass. The criteria will include speed of processing under light, normal and heavy workloads, accuracy, ability to detect and respond appropriately to error conditions and the input or production of invalid data;

(g) system management requirements — detailed specifications of the levels of customer support, maintenance (routine and emergency), and performance testing and monitoring;

(h) contractual requirements — any aspects which might be subject to special conditions: an example of this would be a stipulation about the national origin of equipment;

(i) background information about the operating environment relevant to the operation of the system — this should include a description of the current system, its scope and method of operation and appropriate statistics;

(j) references — a listing of all documents referred to in the specification. This may include documents from the analysis stage and feasibility study, references to technical literature, suppliers data, and technical standards. In view of the growing awareness of the need for careful design of features such as screen displays and the pattern of responses between the user and the machine, references to established good practice and example systems may be included.

Notes

1   Based on sections 4.4 and 4.9 of Brookes, C. H. P. *et al.*, *Information systems design*, Sydney, Prentice-Hall, 1982.
2   Fiedler, F. E. and Chemers, M. 'M., *Leadership and effective management*, New York, Scott-Foresman, 1974.

3   Based on Sections 3.6.4 to 3.6.7 of Abbott, R. J., *An integrated approach to software development*, New York, Wiley, 1986.

4   Based on Section 3.6.8 of Abbott, R. J., *An integrated approach to software development*, New York, Wiley, 1986.

6 *Implementation and evaluation*

Introduction

There is no general agreement amongst writers and analysts as to what is covered during the stage of implementation. Some prefer to describe implementation as the stage during which a tested design, for which equipment has been purchased, is installed, staff trained and the new system set to work. Others prefer to describe implementation as including the acquisition of equipment, materials and software, installation and training, followed by start-up of the new system. Throughout this chapter the second definition will be assumed.

The stages of implementation may be broadly defined as:

- system procurement
- reorganization strategy
- staff training
- testing
- public relations
- 'start-up'

The precise details of stages, in particular the emphasis given to each, will depend on the project and several stages may run in parallel.

Implementation is the penultimate step in the system life cycle. It is the stage at which the commitment by management to the introduction of a new system is expressed in a decision to seek a supplier: the conceptual is to become actual. This represents another point, therefore, where a brief review of the project should be undertaken. As with previous reviews, the main point to be resolved is whether the objectives of the project still meet the needs of users, as currently perceived. If the project has been in progress for a long time, say several months, it is almost certain that there will be some differences. Even though great care may have been taken to try to include changes in the perceived user needs as they became evident to the analyst and design team it is unlikely that this will have been completely achieved. Some expectations entertained by users may have proved, on analysis, not capable of being fulfilled within the resources available to the library or information service. Some may have required technological developments beyond those currently available. It is useful to keep a record of these together with the reasons for not pursuing them. A final look by the management team through the list will ensure that no significant and possible suggestion or request has been overlooked. Thereafter the list can form the basis for further development or re-design of the system. The list also serves as a record that serious consideration has been given to all evident user needs.

As a project proceeds through the stages of the system life cycle, there is an increasing commitment of resources: from problem recognition to feasibility study and analysis, on to design, the transfer from one stage to another faces the manager with the question: proceed and commit further resources, or stop? It is easy to be swept along with enthusiasm, coupled with the notion that stopping will mean the loss of resources already invested in the project. This reasoning is, however, largely fallacious: resources, especially money, which have already been used cannot be recovered if they have been employed to fund intangibles such as design work. They represent a 'sunk cost'. The manager must concentrate on the use of resources in the future and the only appropriate decision is whether the *incremental* cost arising from proceeding can be justified when compared with other options for the use of those resources. This is not to neglect the social consequences of cancelling a project, especially at a late stage, but the manager must be clear that the main decision is about the use of resources.

By this stage in the system life cycle any lingering doubts about the perceived value of the project and its objectives should have been assuaged. Participative approaches to analysis and design tend to be very useful in encouraging a free exchange of views. Nevertheless, there are several examples of projects which have been scrapped at a late stage because they have drifted so far from their original objectives that the benefit to the organization and users from their continuance was not perceived as being sufficient. Often, the failure of management to conduct adequate and timely reviews allows such drift to occur. At a later stage, management becomes aware of the changed nature of the project and is then launched into precipitate action, leading to panic and bad feeling.

The stage of implementation represents another crucial time, or

155

'breakpoint', at which the decision to proceed with a further commitment of resources should be made after review.

Managerial attitudes

There are two contrasting and sometimes contradictory strands of endeavour in implementation: the satisfaction of human requirements and the establishment of a system technology which works. The managerial component in both strands is large, but rather different in character. With the first strand, that of satisfying human requirements, the manager is principally involved in negotiations with staff and users: those who are usually already part of the internal and operating environments. Unless new or very insensitive, the manager should already be aware of the range of anxieties, expectations and needs expressed by the staff and should be alert to user needs too. Participative techniques can certainly help in the gathering of this information, whereas there is a danger of it being overlooked if only hard systems methodologies are in use. It is easy to become so involved in technical matters that simple consideration of the feelings of others, their hopes and aspirations and pride in the job they do, are neglected.

The extent to which detailed consideration should be given to these factors depends on the anticipated impact of the project and its novelty. The implementation of an upgraded cataloguing system using a standard software package would, for example, have an impact on several staff, especially those responsible for record creation. Users may be unaware of its introduction because the appearance of the catalogue records might remain substantially the same. The novelty of the project would be low and its impact localized. Implementation could be planned without extensive consultations, except with those involved with record creation. On the other hand, the introduction of an automated system into a library or information service with no prior experience of the use of computers would have a major impact on staff and users and would constitute a novel experience. Implementation strategies would need to be discussed to minimize disruption and to ease learning.

However routine and small scale the project might appear to be it is important that implementation be carefully planned. Staff and users need time to absorb and learn about even apparently trivial changes. The introduction of a new word-processing program might seem a very minor change but its learning will present a challenge to all potential users and a major learning experience for those without previous knowledge of such applications.

156

The problem is often compounded by managerial attitudes which arise from long familiarity with a project. It is easy to forget the confusion of the early days of the project, the uncertainties and the misunderstandings. It is easy to forget the extent of the learning experience undergone by the analyst and designers as the project has evolved. It is altogether too easy to underestimate the difficulty those outside the project team may encounter in trying to understand why a particular approach has been adopted or why a particular technology has been chosen. Patience and a carefully designed training programme will help in the change to new methods; adequate time to adapt is a major need.

System procurement

The system specification will form the basis of the tenders to be solicited from potential suppliers. The process of seeking tenders has been fully described by Corbin[1] for the North American market and briefly explained by Lovecy[2] in the context of the United Kingdom.

A tender is an offer, or proposal, by a manufacturer to supply goods or services made on the basis of an invitation by a prospective customer. It is a formal process used when the intended purchase is expensive, complicated or large. For simpler purchases, for example a microcomputer, a customer would, in most cases, scan the market using advertisements, product reviews and other sources to draw up a short list of suitable products. In both cases the system specification should play an important part because it can be used to identify two important sets of factors: mandatory requirements and desirable features.

Mandatory requirements are those things which are vital to the successful working of the system. They are the foundation without which the system cannot meet the needs of the library or information service. A product or service which does not meet these requirements will be considered unacceptable. The requirements may be tangible or they may be qualities. Examples, for an automated system, might be a training programme run by the vendor for staff to become familiar with the new equipment, a defined minimum speed of processing, capacity to support a certain number of terminals and an adequate level of servicing and maintenance.

Desirable features are those things which have been identified in the system specification as being important but their omission would not compromise the new system. In selecting a product, having eliminated those which do not meet the mandatory requirements, it is the extent to which each meets the defined list of desirable features that will form the main criterion for choice.

Careful consideration should be given to establishing the list of mandatory requirements and desirable features. It is easy to become so bemused by brochures and sales patter that a product may be bought on the basis of the features to which the maker wants to draw attention rather than a sober assessment of whether it meets the needs of the library or information service. Additional features – 'nice to have' features – can certainly be considered as part of the process of choice but the proper time is after having been satisfied that the mandatory requirements can be met and that all the desirable features are present. Products which meet these criteria can then be compared by examining the additional features.

If the project is not large enough to warrant using the tendering process the list of mandatory requirements and desirable features can be used to select a suitable product. In making a choice some consideration should be given to reputation of the supplier, if this can be ascertained. Unfortunately, the market for some products, especially computer products and software, is comparatively new and many companies rise and fade away quite quickly. There is always a risk attached to purchase and managers should take this into account when making a choice of product. It is possible to reduce the risk by making enquiries about companies, seeking previous customers and reading the trade press; these measures should certainly be taken if the product is expected to be used for a long time, during which period it may require support and maintenance by the manufacturer. On the other hand, some exciting and innovative products are likely to be offered by new companies: to neglect these because of an absence of track record might result in an interesting opportunity being forgone. There is one particular difficulty which may be encountered with new products, especially those from the computer and software industry: companies will sometimes advertise products well ahead of the production date and a misleading impression of availability may be created. The only safe course is to refuse to consider purchase until an acceptable working version of a product is available.

If tenders are to be invited the prospective suppliers must be provided with a standard set of information about the required product. The system specification is a vital component to which should be added a list of mandatory requirements and desirable features and a timetable outlining the deadlines for implementing the new system. In addition there may be additional information required from manufacturers, such as statements about their policy on product enhancements and development, national origin of components, arrangements for servicing and maintenance and so on. A questionnaire may be included to elicit information about suitable conditions for the use of equipment, such as the need for power supplies, humidity and temperature control, and adequate floor strength. If appropriate, the acceptability of site inspections and presentations by the prospective supplier about the product can be noted and rules for their conduct outlined. If there are special conditions attached to payment, such as the use of payment in stages as work proceeds, penalties for late delivery or partial retention of final payment until the expiry of a 'running-in' period, these should be explained. It is of great help in comparing tenders if potential suppliers can be persuaded to follow a uniform layout in presenting them: a list of headings can be suggested. This is especially important when referring to costings; in the absence of a uniform layout the comparison of costs can become extremely difficult. Finally, there should be a set of instructions to the supplier about the completion and submission of the tender: date for submission, address for delivery and the name of a contact in the organization who can answer any queries which might arise. It is often helpful for the 'request to tender' documents to be prepared by a small team and widely reviewed, thus reducing the risk that some important element will be overlooked.

In selecting potential suppliers it is useful to carry out some initial screening. There is clearly no point in inviting or examining bids from companies that cannot meet the design specifications. A first step in seeking bids is to look closely at the background of companies to determine their experience, track record (do they, for example, have a good reputation for meeting deadlines?) and financial security. The library and information science literature is often a good source of descriptions of installed systems: this should suggest some names of previous customers to approach for an opinion.

Published balance sheets and statements to shareholders (often conveniently summarized by the Extel service), together with surveys by the leading financial newspapers (if larger companies are being considered) may give clues about the performance of companies. Essentially, one is seeking a company which is both run successfully and is in a sound financial position.

The performance of a company is determined by how well it is using the various funds under its control: 'return on net assets' (sometimes called 'return on capital employed') relates profit earned, before tax and interest on long-term loans are paid, to the net assets used in the business:

$$\frac{\text{profit before interest and tax}}{\text{net assets}}$$

Net assets, or 'capital employed', refers to the fixed assets of the company plus its working capital. The capital may arise from funds invested by shareholders, long and short-term debt and reserves built up from trading in previous years. A company may raise its return on net assets ratio by increasing the revenue from its trading or by reducing the expenses it incurs in business. Sound marketing, effective design and research, good after-sales services may all help to increase sales whilst skilful purchasing and regular care and maintenance of plant may reduce the use of fixed assets.

Measuring the financial status of a company depends upon judging how well it can meet its liabilities. A company incurs liabilities in the form of both long-term liabilities such as debts repayable over several years and short-term liabilities, the repayment of which will fall due within one year. Examples of short-term liabilities are the payment of tax, creditors and dividends to shareholders. It is important, therefore, to establish that a company is both solvent — able to meet its long-term liabilities — and has sufficient liquidity to cover its short-term liabilities.

Solvency can be judged from the 'debt ratio':

$$\frac{\text{long term loans (debt)}}{\text{capital employed}}$$

A low debt ratio indicates a high level of cover should such debts become immediately repayable. Of equal concern is whether the company can pay the interest on such debts. This is revealed by the 'interest cover' ratio:

$$\frac{\text{profit before interest and tax}}{\text{loan interest}}$$

A high interest cover ratio indicates safety in the payment of these liabilities.

Liquidity is also measured with two ratios: the current ratio and the 'acid test', or liquidity, ratio. The current ratio demonstrates to what extent short-term assets are available to cover short-term liabilities:

$$\frac{\text{current assets}}{\text{current liabilities}}$$

If this ratio is less than one, it shows that the company is not in a position to meet its short-term liabilities from the cash or other assets (such as stock and money owed to the company by debtors) which may be quickly converted into cash. This may indicate that a problem is developing and is certainly worthy of attention. The 'acid test' ratio provides the strictest test of liquidity:

$$\frac{\text{liquid assets (current assets less stock)}}{\text{current liabilities}}$$

By excluding stock from the calculation of the ratio, due account is taken of the fact that it may take several months to convert such assets into cash. This ratio shows, therefore, the ability of a company to meet an immediate call for payment. It is not unusual for this ratio to be less than one but, if it is, the company will need to be careful about its short-term cash planning.

A measure of the market assessment of a company is often useful: for a company quoted on the Stock Exchange, the price/earnings ratio:

$$\frac{\text{market price per ordinary share}}{\text{earnings per ordinary share after tax}}$$

is a broad measure of market assessment. The higher the ratio, the greater the regard for the company.

These ratios can have meaning in two ways: by comparison of the same company over time or the comparison of several companies over the same period of time. For this to be a sensible procedure it is necessary that similar and consistent accounting practices should have been used during the period of comparison. The problems are further discussed by Reid and Myddelton.[3] If a large contract is to be placed with a company it is worth seeking a professional opinion of the company from a financial analyst.

For proposed very large systems, or those involving novel approaches, it may be difficult to identify candidate suppliers. The best course is to approach companies which have already demonstrated an ability to work on projects of a similar scale and type and invite them to comment on whether the specification could be met by modification of their existing products within nine months to one year and whether they would be willing to undertake such modification. If the system specification cannot be met by product modification, they should be invited to consider undertaking full development of the specified system as a new product.

161

Both approaches involve a much higher degree of risk than the purchase of an existing product. It is essential that the specification should include clear statements about the required performance of the proposed system under conditions of normal and expected maximum load; in addition, the timetable for installation of the new system should be clearly defined. The essential point is to ensure that a prospective vendor is clear about the obligations attendant upon being awarded the contract.

Some prospective suppliers may indicate an interest in supplying the required system but be unable to meet the specification in full. A typical instance would be an inability to supply the system by the specified deadline. The library or information service manager must recognize that commercial realities encourage firms to maintain full order books and the lead time for supply of new systems can become long. Some negotiation may be possible if a short delay is not thought likely to compromise the success of the project. When comparing tenders, however, it will be important to bear in mind that a condition of the system specification has not been completely satisfied. If a rival company can meet the specification in all respects, including the development timetable, then it will be a stronger candidate for the award of the contract.

The comparison of tenders should be facilitated by the request to prospective suppliers to submit them according to a uniform pattern. If this has not happened then some time should be spent in abstracting the various elements from each tender to build up a table allowing comparison of ability to meet mandatory requirements and supply desirable features, costings, ability to meet timetables and additional information about each company, such as experience and reputation. Vendors not meeting the mandatory requirements can be excluded from further consideration. Thereafter, the comparison is based on an objective consideration of costs and system features. If appropriate, the comparison of costs should encompass initial purchase costs and running costs over several years. An important consideration if the system involves computers or other advanced technology is the availability of servicing and maintenance: a competent local servicing representative backed by adequate supplies is clearly an advantage. Satisfactory proposals for dealing with 'out of hours' emergencies should be made, together with arrangements for routine servicing which will minimize disruption of the day-to-day operations of the system. Subjective matters such as the impression given by company representatives, publicity and opinions held by previous customers should be taken into consideration but are best dealt with after an initial selection of suppliers has been made. Subjective matters are also best considered by a group to ensure that a balanced view emerges. The selection process should result in the award of a contract to one of the companies which have tendered for supply. It is occasionally necessary to conclude that none of the tenders is entirely satisfactory because there is a gap between the required performance of a proposed system and what is promised by manufacturers. The library or information service managers must then consider whether to extend the tendering process to other potential suppliers (those, perhaps, outside the group well known for this kind of work), revise the system requirements to achieve a better match with the proposals received or to seek to negotiate with the suppliers whose proposals come closest to the stated requirements. Each option is risky, though the latter two represent low-risk strategies unless the proposals of the suppliers fall far short of user expectations.

Moving to suppliers outside the usual range may prove very successful, especially if a company is keen to enter a new market, but the company's lack of experience of the product and the market may lead it to be over-ambitious, especially towards meeting deadlines. Before accepting a tender, the library or information service managers should seek assurances that sufficient resources are at the disposal of the company to fund any necessary research and development. In addition, the library or information service may have to undertake an educative role if the personnel of the company are to appreciate the nature of the work which the system is intended to support. If this role is significant it may be possible to negotiate a reduction in the overall price charged for the system in recognition of the development effort of the library or information service. A close working relationship may result and this can lead to the production of a system which meets the needs of users very well.

Having agreed on a supplier, the next step is to accept the tender, subject to any points of clarification or negotiation which may have emerged during the comparison exercise, and enter into a contract. Because this represents the point at which a legal agreement will be entered into it is vital that appropriate professional advice be sought. For many library or information services this aspect will be covered by the legal departments of the parent organization. It is still important, however, for the managers of the library or information service to be involved in reviewing the conditions of the contract. The purpose of any contract is to protect the interests of the supplier; the purchaser must

163

ensure that the obligations on both sides are clear and unambiguous. A contract may need to be negotiated clause by clause and altered to ensure that it is fair. Matthews[4] discusses the contract in some detail in the context of automated systems in the United States; the outlines he offers for both supply and maintenance contracts form a useful basis for assessing contracts for other kinds of purchase and within other jurisdictions.

A vital section of the contract relates to the test procedures which will be used to determine whether the system will meet the specified requirements. In particular, standards of throughput and working capacity should be included, together with tests for reliability of equipment and ability to meet the various requirements for validation and the correct response to error conditions. The tests should include a range of on-site checks carried out after installation is complete as well as tests carried out in the factory. The tests will already have been described in some detail in the system specification but should also be mentioned in the contract to underline their importance. If a modular system is being specified, with each component having its own set of test procedures, an overall test of the system should also be specified to ensure that it will work satisfactorily under conditions of full load with all components or subsystems working to capacity. Payment for the development of modular systems should, if possible, be made in stages as each module passes its tests.

'Good faith' is an admirable characteristic of many human relationships. There is no reason to suppose that suppliers are necessarily mendacious but the library or information service manager must recognize the nature of a commercial agreement. Oral agreements and understanding should be translated into written statements, preferably as part of the contract. If something is vital to the success of a project, installation to meet a particular date, for example, then this must be specified and made the 'essence of the contract': the implication for the parties to the contract is that the contract is broken if this particular condition is not met. Equally, the contract will specify obligations for the library or information service: the supplier may want unrestricted access to buildings on particular dates for the purposes of installation, for example, and this may necessitate temporary closure or restriction of normal library services.

Reorganization strategy

Having negotiated and signed the contract for the new system there may

164

be an understandable wish by the management team to relax, feeling that the work is now in the hands of the supplier. There is, however, much to be done. In particular, a strategy for reorganization needs to be developed. This is an apt moment for such work because the discussions leading up to the signing of the contract will have alerted participants and others as to the nature of the change and there will be a motivational drive to react in some way. The danger is that if this 'free energy' is not harnessed for the benefit of the project it may be dissipated in worry, resistance to the aims of the project and the defence of previous methods of working. In many instances there will be a gap of several weeks or months between the placing of the order and installation of the new system. The aim of the management team should be to fill this by turning the attention of staff (and, if appropriate, users of the service) towards the need to assimilate new ideas and methods of working. Opportunities for the discussion of potential problems, ideas and other concerns should be created; information about the new system should be shared. In this way enthusiasm for the new system will be generated and sustained; residual worries and resentment will have a channel for their expression and can thus be discharged.

A first step in developing a reorganization strategy is to identify the functional groups within the internal environment and any user groups in the operating environment which will be affected by the implementation of the new system. Members from some of these groups may already have been consulted as part of the analysis and design stages of the project; members from each group should now form an implementation team. To the team should be added members of other groups which represent sources of appropriate special expertise: if the project will necessitate building alterations, for example, then members from the maintenance department should be nominated. It is unlikely that the 'specialist' members will wish to attend all meetings, preferring, perhaps, to be invited when concerns in their particular areas are to be discussed. It is important that they be invited to early meetings of the team where the outlines of the reorganization strategy are to be determined and, thereafter, that they are kept informed of the business of the meetings and changes which might affect timetables for implementation and resource allocation. The implementation team should be encouraged to form sub-groups to consider particular needs such as staff training.

For the control of a large project it may be necessary to form an additional steering committee, consisting of senior management, to review reports on progress from the implementation team and to coordinate the use of resources. The function of this steering committee is to provide overall leadership as implementation proceeds and to act as an arbiter in case of disagreements. There is some merit in restricting the establishment of committees and concentrating the work of implementation in a small team with an effective leader. Such a group should become strongly task-oriented because the objectives and constraints will rapidly become clear and because the various crises and uncertainties which arise during implementation will call for firm and fast decision-making. A hierarchy of steering committees, working groups and sub-groups can rapidly become self-serving as formal procedures, bound to an agenda, replace thought and action.

Whatever control structure is eventually decided upon, it is important that a formal review procedure be established to ensure that progress is noted at regular intervals and adjustments made to resource allocation. The essence of implementation is contained in the timetable: suppliers and purchasers are working to dates already agreed and built into the contract. It is the main work of the implementation team to ensure that these dates are met.

Staff training

The reorganization programme should include staff training as a major component. The first step in staff training will be to inform all staff (not just those in the departments affected by the new system) of the development of a new system, the objectives set for it, criteria for choice and the timetable for its implementation. Thereafter, staff training should concentrate on exploring the ways in which the new system will affect existing patterns of work and assisting staff to gain the necessary skills to use new equipment and processes. The aim is to bring everyone to a state of awareness sufficient for them to be able to work satisfactorily from the inception of the new system.

Curiosity about the new system will be high immediately after the initial announcement. The training programme should be designed to channel this interest into learning. Participants need to feel secure about the tasks to which they have been assigned and able to carry them out. Training needs to be specifically addressed to the requirements of each task but must also include an understanding of the complete system sufficient for participants to appreciate the relationship between their jobs, the jobs of others and the operation of the complete system. In this way, the importance of the contribution of each task to the overall effectiveness of the system is easier to discern. Compilers of bibliographic records need, for example, to recognize that successful retrieval from an online public access catalogue will largely depend on the decisions they have made. To be avoided is a programme which splits processes into separate tasks, trains participants intensively on one or more tasks and then unleashes them on to the new system unaware of what others are doing. Training by suppliers often falls into this category. Whilst it is convenient to use such facilities, and may be essential if the new system adopts novel procedures or uses newly developed equipment, it should occupy a place within a training programme which also provides a wider perspective. Visits to other sites or library or information services already operating with similar systems can often prove valuable in enhancing this perception.

Opportunities for staff reaction and the making of suggestions should also form part of the training programme. It is helpful if a representative of senior management is present at these sessions to give participants confidence that their ideas will receive attention; it is essential that considered feedback about the utility of these ideas be given. Failure to listen and respond in due time will quickly lead to a decline in enthusiasm and a loss of motivation.

A staff newsletter is a valuable adjunct to a training programme. It can form an effective way of keeping staff informed of progress, announcing developments and changes and provide a forum for debating problems and exchanging experience.

Manuals describing the working of the system should be supplied by the manufacturers; these are rarely an adequate substitute for an 'in-house' manual produced to support and complement the training programme. Manuals from suppliers often assume prior technical knowledge and may be written in a style which is painful if not incomprehensible. An 'in-house' manual should describe the system which has been installed and should relate the necessary technical descriptions to local conditions. It is also important to appreciate that few people relish reading manuals: the tendency on receiving one is to glance at it and then set it aside for later study: thereafter, it remains unread. People prefer, in the main, to gain information about new procedures by watching and asking others. Only when colleagues cannot answer a technical question will someone turn, in desperation, to the manual. Therefore, the writer of a staff manual ought to have two objectives. The first is to ensure that a brief initial skim through the contents should be as fruitful as possible: how to get into the system and, equally important, how to get out again, followed by a brief point-by-point description of what the system will do should occupy the preliminary pages. Following this there should be a more detailed outline, perhaps using a flowchart, showing the relationship of all the procedures and a reference to the detailed description of each to be found in the remainder of the manual. Names and locations for further advice should be given. A full index, together with 'tabbed' separators, will assist in the achievement of the second objective, that of providing a quick source of assistance. The most important test for a draft text of any manual is for it to be given to staff unfamiliar with the system and to gauge their reactions as they try to use it.

Manuals should always carry a compilation date and version number; if it is a loose-leaf manual, where the intention is to issue additions and corrections for insertion into a binder, this information should be repeated on each page. A separate sheet for recording the insertion of amendments and deletions is also useful as a means of checking that the information in a copy is up-to-date.

The training programme should be evaluated both immediately after its conclusion and later in relation to the experience of participants with the full, working system. This latter stage of evaluation can also offer useful insights into the construction of a permanent training package which can be used for the indoctrination of new staff. Experience will also suggest aspects of training which can be included in a refresher course for existing staff: parts of the initial training will be forgotten, especially if some of the techniques covered are little used, and some evidence of unintentional misuse of the system may emerge. Useful short-cuts, means of overcoming problems and effective emergency procedures will also become evident; improvements and enhancements to the system by the supplier will become available. To designate one or more persons to be in charge of the maintenance of a training programme and staff manuals is the best way of ensuring that all such ideas and developments are taken into account.

Testing
Two aspects of testing are important at this stage: testing the components of the system against the specifications stated by the supplier and testing the system against the requirements defined in the system specification.

'Benchmarks' are often used by manufacturers to test components. The procedure is to establish a standard routine, or set of routines, which the component must be able to process satisfactorily according to some criterion such as completing the job within a set period of time. The use of benchmarks is widespread: for example, within the computer industry there are several benchmark programs which can be used to compare equipment. It is the task of the supplier to be satisfied that each component of a system is operating to a satisfactory standard.

The system specification defines required levels of performance for the system, validation routines and required procedures under error conditions. These set the 'benchmarks' for system performance but their assessment will necessitate the creation of a set of test routines. The system must be tested under conditions of the specified maximum work load to ensure that it can cope. If testing a computer-assisted system, for example, a satisfactory response time from the system must be obtainable when all terminals are in use simultaneously. A test program must be devised, using flows of data typical of those to be encountered in reality, to simulate this condition. The documentation from the analysis and design stages and the system specification should be studied carefully to determine what ranges of data are considered acceptable, points during processing at which error conditions could occur and the procedure to be followed in dealing with the error. If, for example, a computer-assisted acquisitions system is being tested, how should it respond to the input of a negative number in the 'price' field of a record? The testing program should include examples of valid and invalid data formats, out-of-range items and data which exceeds or does not fill its allocated field space. The effect of data being absent from a field should be checked. Editing and correction routines must be tested. Output should also be checked to ensure that correct error messages are displayed and that procedures for recovery from this position work.

The process of testing is vital to the success of the system. The process should be devised with care, carried out by the suppliers under supervision and the results scrutinized. Any deficiencies should be identified and a report made to the system suppliers. It is then for the library or information service managers to decide to accept the system or to ask for modifications to bring it up to the specification. Some negotiation may be possible. For example, it may be thought inconvenient to reject a system because of some error which has little consequence for overall operations; provided the suppliers undertake to correct the fault within an agreed period, the system could be accepted.

Public relations
The user groups which the library or information service aims to serve should also be considered as part of the implementation programme. They represent one of the stakeholders to be found in the operating environment

169

and they, along with other stakeholders, ought to be kept informed about the implementation of the new system. In this way the new system is more likely to be accepted and this can be an important factor in its success especially if the new system directly affects those parts of the service with which users habitually have contact. To introduce radical changes, even if they *will* lead to a better service, without preparing the users is to invite trouble.

As a first step use should be made of whatever local community information services exist to inform users that a change is imminent, explain the reasons for the change, the anticipated improvements to the performance of the system, and suggest what, if anything, users will need to do to make use of the new system. Local broadcasting and newspapers provide efficient means of reaching a large and dispersed user group; the material to be released should be very carefully prepared to prevent concentration on one issue (often the failures of the previous system) by reporters seeking a minor sensation. The material should also be interesting: concentrating on the main topics and not providing a wealth of detail is more likely to catch the editor's eye. The detail should be held back for use in an explanatory leaflet.

Material, such as leaflets, for distribution to users should repeat the basic outline of information about the new system and then explain in more detail how the user will be affected. Care should be taken not to 'oversell' the system, especially if it uses novel approaches or is very complex. New systems *will* have teething troubles and users can quickly become sceptical about the advertised advantages.

Training of library or information service users may be useful and, indeed, necessary if the new system will change the public aspects of the service. Users may have to become accustomed to new arrangements, stationery and procedures. This should be explained as the time for changeover to the new system draws near. It is best not to do this too soon, however, or the impact is lost. Displays and demonstrations can draw attention to the changes and provide a point of contact for feedback from users. There may be complaints and staff will need some training in how to deal with them. Senior management should seek to be informed about complaints because a discernible pattern may emerge, indicating the need to adjust procedures or take special precautions. A sensitive approach is needed if incidents are to be dealt with satisfactorily and ill feeling assuaged.

A public relations exercise can be continued after the implementation: users may be interested in how successful the new system is judged to be and may wish to be informed of what improvements may be expected. It is also useful to provide feedback on the progress towards following up suggestions or criticisms.

Conversion

The changeover from the old to the new system or the start of a novel system is a difficult and risky time. If the system is large and in the public eye, breakdown or failure will be embarrassing and detrimental to the political interests of the library or information service. Changeover should be planned with great care and detailed consideration should be given to appropriate recovery procedures when failures occur. The system tests, if they have been conducted properly, will reduce the risk of failure but there remains a fairly large probability that some breakdowns will occur. Contingency plans, thoroughly understood and rehearsed by staff, are vital to successful changeover.

Some work on changeover may have to be undertaken quite early in the implementation programme. It is frequently the case that records will need to be converted, especially if a computer-assisted system is being installed. Many of the records used in libraries and information services present particular problems. Catalogue records, in particular, tend to be lengthy and complex in structure. Because the catalogue has, in many cases, been built up over several years there may be inconsistencies, especially if several people have worked on record creation or if successive versions of a cataloguing code have been in use. Editing will often be essential if the new database is to be of acceptable quality. It may be possible to purchase records from an existing database to supplement or replace incomplete records but the editing process will still represent a major and expensive commitment.

Some consideration should be given to options other than complete conversion of the existing catalogue. The most drastic is not to convert it but to close the old catalogue and start afresh. This option has been pursued by many libraries, often accompanied by plans for conversion of the old catalogue when funds eventually permit. Commercial companies will also undertake the conversion process but strict editing procedures must be established and quality control procedures specified. Other options to total conversion are conversion only of records which are in use and partial conversion − splitting the old catalogue at a certain date or according to some other criterion.

Whatever option is chosen, realistic estimates of the time necessary for conversion should be made. Make some allowance for delays and interruptions and it should not be assumed that an optimal work rate can be maintained day after day. Record conversion needs to be planned carefully; a procedure manual is a useful means of maintaining consistency of procedures and training other staff.

The other aspect of conversion is the procedure to be adopted for changeover from the old to the new system. Four methods are commonly used and represent different levels of risk. The safest is parallel running of the old and the new systems for a limited time. For a computer-assisted system this implies that data will be processed by both systems and the results carefully checked. In the event of system malfunction the integrity of the service is maintained. This option is expensive and can only be justified where service quality must not be compromised.

Pilot running uses the new system to rerun data already processed by the old system. This allows a further opportunity to check the operation of the new system under 'live' conditions and offers a low level of risk.

A phased changeover allows a gradual transfer of processing from the old to the new systems. For a short time the systems are allowed to run in parallel and, when it is apparent that the new system can cope, work is gradually transferred. The risk of failure is moderate. Phased changeover is especially suitable if a system consists of several modules: these can be brought successively into use.

Direct changeover is the most risky strategy: the old system is abandoned and all processing is switched to the new. This may be suitable for systems whose failure would have a minor effect on services but should otherwise be avoided unless there is great confidence that the new system will work as expected.

Whatever changeover strategy is adopted, contingency plans for system failure *must* be established.

The period of the changeover needs careful planning to ensure that all staff know what is expected of them and are sufficiently well informed as to be able to assist users who may be confused by the new system. Special attention should be given to the provision of clear notices and someone should be on hand to answer questions or to sort out problems. How long this special provision should continue depends on the magnitude of the change as it affects the users: for changeover to a new circulation control system, for example, it would be wise to continue until a full issue period has elapsed, at least. The standard for which to aim is clear, consistent, guidance readily available when needed but otherwise unobtrusive.

Evaluation

The library or information service which ends up with a system which works efficiently, as specified, and to the satisfaction of all is very fortunate. A more realistic expectation is that the compromises introduced during the design stage and the experience of implementation will highlight areas where the system itself, or its manner of introduction, fall short of complete acceptability. If the work involved in the analysis and design stages has been carried out carefully there should not be major discontent or evidence of failure.

Evaluation, as part of the operation stage of the system life cycle, is a step which is often omitted or forgotten. Immediately after the implementation there is a downturn of motivation, a sense of tiredness, even depression. This is quite understandable, because any project requires a large input of physical and mental energy if it is to produce anything. Also, commitment tends to grow as the project proceeds and the roles of participants become clearer. On the other hand, if the matter is left for a long time, then interest will have moved on to other things, and it may be difficult to divert energy to this evaluation. A useful approach may be to carry out two evaluations: one immediately after the implementation to discuss the project management and organization, working relationships and so on. This should be done fairly swiftly, because memories of feelings soon fade. After some period of stable working, then is the point where an evaluation of the new system should be undertaken, comparing its performance under peak and typical conditions with the expected performance characteristics. It is almost certain that there will be some discrepancy, either because of unanticipated circumstances or because the system is being used in slightly different way than was originally conceived. This kind of drift in operating procedure is entirely to be expected as staff discover the short cuts or ways around obstacles to what they want to do. Observe and analyse: then compare with user needs. If there is a large discrepancy, then one is back at the start of the system life cycle, recognizing an opportunity of improving service to the user. Often fine-tuning is all that is called for to ensure a system which continues to be satisfactory.

The post-implementation evaluation has another purpose: to determine whether the installed system is as defined in the contract. Deficiencies may be identified which should be rectified at the expense of the supplier; the need for eventual modifications may also become evident. Discussion of the implementation strategy and project management is also valuable: there is much to be learned about smoothing the process of

173

implementation.

If possible it is better for the evaluation to be carried out by someone who has not been directly involved with the design team and the planning of the implementation. It is quite difficult for staff and users to give an entirely honest reaction if they know that the person asking has had a major role in introducing the new system. It is also useful for the evaluator to interview members of the design team about the experience of working as a team. Valuable insights about team composition and methods of working may emerge. Users should also be interviewed and a small-scale survey may provide further useful information.

The evaluator is not only concerned with the acceptability of the system and its ability to meet the specification. As part of the study additional areas for development will probably emerge: the expectations of users should have been raised as a result of contact with the new system and this may stimulate them to ask for further refinements. It is necessary to review such suggestions with care before adopting them: even then, each should be subjected to a feasibility study before proceeding.

No system is ever complete. A regular review, perhaps annually, is especially important for an automated system because technological development may supply solutions to any problems which persist. A review directs attention to such matters.

Notes

1   Corbin, J. B., *Managing the library automation project*, Phoenix, Arizona, Oryx, 1985, part III, 'System procurement'.
2   Lovecy, I., *Automating library procedures: a survivor's handbook*, London, Library Association, 1984.
3   Reid, W. and Myddelton, D. R., *The meaning of company accounts*, 2nd ed., London, Gower, 1974.
4   Matthews, J. R., *Choosing an automated library system: a planning guide*, Chicago, Illinois, American Library Association, 1980, chapter 5.

7 *The management of change*

Introduction

The management of change and the success or failure of projects are strongly linked. Parkin[1] discusses the factors which can be held responsible for project failure, but suggests that there may be little to be gained from a lengthy analysis of failed projects. His contention is that such questioning is often of dubious objectivity and likely to result only in the rehearsal of opinion and prejudice. Whilst one can agree that a hindsight view of failure may concentrate on antipathies and discord, it is still possible to argue for some attempt at the study of project failures. Reasons for this contention arise out of a general observation about the systems approach: human behaviour, its foibles and fancies, is an intrinsic part of the system. If one considers the systems approach, it is evident that problems usually occur where one part of a system is linked, or interfaced, with another. Sometimes, the system components are machinery, pure and simple. Machinery, despite what one may suspect, is not malevolent, does not harbour grudges and cannot refuse to cooperate. It can, however, be the product of faulty design, not an appropriate choice for the purpose or incapable of performing to the required specification. All of these problems could account for the failure of a project, but they are attributable to human failings rather than intrinsic to the machinery. Moreover, there is no way that machinery can be persuaded to change, or to do better. Similarly, consider the specification of a process: design flaws here could contribute to project failure, but those flaws are attributable to lack of care or understanding by humans. Machinery and, to extend the idea, all systems, bear the mark of their creator: whatever the systems can do and how they do it is ultimately a reflection of us, our concerns and interests and our weaknesses. Project failures are attributable solely to human error.

Project management must be concerned with the control of human

175

resources to reduce the level of error, to detect and correct errors and to anticipate where error may significantly affect the likelihood of success. At the same time, it must be admitted that many developments have taken place because people have erred: they have done something unexpected and beyond what was required of them. Creativity and control do not sit easily together; the sensitive manager recognizes what can be gained from a creative approach, but is also aware that uncontrolled experimentation can be costly and can easily go well beyond the areas of interest of the organization. One cannot argue against the merits of a creative approach in the workplace in general, or within the confines of a project, but some control and direction is needed. Control is concerned with comparing cost and benefits and is primarily concerned with the efficient use of resources, whilst strategic management is concerned with deciding what the benefits might be and assigning them some value in relation to user needs. To put it another way, at the level of strategic management judgement is not solely in terms of costs and benefits, but extends to comparing costs and satisfaction of needs. It is concerned with the effective use of resources. Proper and useful project control must be concerned with costs, benefits and effectiveness.

This is not to suggest that the project manager should concentrate solely on what can be measured or on attempting to represent in measurable form what cannot otherwise be measured. The suggestion that 'hard' management information — that is, numerical information such as statistics, and costs and benefits expressed in monetary terms — is the only type of management information worth collecting should make any manager uneasy. Consider the awe in which financial information, and figures generally, are held, even by quite senior managers. Such data has the aura of objectivity, it seems precise and factual, but a careful study of resource management techniques will indicate that the presentation of management information includes a measure of subjective judgement. There is no obviously 'right' way to allocate project costs, for example. Such costs could be borne centrally as an overhead of the business in general, or they might be divided over the departments most immediately affected. The decision requires judgement about present conditions and the future if the best decision for the good of the organization is to be made. Such decisions cannot be objective because they involve speculation. In assessing the costs of a project running over several years one may be guided by the state of the money market, economic forecasts and best commercial practice but, in the end, someone makes a guess about the future. Even the presentation of financial information in the form of accounts involves some subjectivity. Most published sets of accounts will contain sets of notes explaining why particular accounting conventions have been adopted. The professional accounting standards may suggest what is good practice for many areas where differing procedures might be used, but complete specification is not possible.

If there is subjectivity in such a seemingly cut-and-dried area, then one should certainly be aware of it when approaching the shifting sands of benefit assessments or judgements about effectiveness. There may be debate about the nature and scale of a benefit but discussion should lead to a collective opinion where several subjective views are pooled. The result is still subjective, of course. Trying to impute monetary value to benefits introduces another subjective factor because the comparative value of benefits is very much a matter of judgement.

Many of the measures used are subjective but they can be used provided everyone understands what they represent and what they cannot represent. There remains a danger: once things are represented in numerical terms, people tend to argue and debate as if the figures do represent reality, rather than a subjective approximation. This is not an argument for rejecting such information but, rather, one for using it in full knowledge of how it has been derived.

Sources of conflict during projects

If there is a mystique about the cost−benefit approach to assessing projects, it is enshrined in the process of recognizing what the costs and benefits actually are and how they have been determined. In preceding chapters the point has been made that the satisfactory control of a project depends on deciding at successive points throughout the life of the project whether or not it is worth going on: will the expected benefits justify the anticipated expenditure? Several factors can distort perception of costs and benefits and thus lead to conflict.

Major sources of conflict are identified below, together with suggestions for avoidance or resolution. The list[2] is not exhaustive and must, in practice, be modified to suit the scale and objectives of each project.

Conflict over project priorities

Managers should seek to establish clearly defined plans during the project planning stage and encourage participative management and joint decision-making. It is also important to stress the importance of the project to the goals of the organization. During the life of the project the management team should provide effective feedback about forecasts and progress to each part of the organization affected by the project.

Conflict over administrative procedures
Develop, in some detail, administrative procedures for the management and control of the project and secure approval for these procedures from key administrators whose resources are affected by the project. As the project proceeds, develop contingency plans for future stages, to allow for reallocation of resources if there is need.

Conflict over technical opinions and performance trade-offs
Attempt the early resolution of emerging technical problems. It is important to ensure technical staff are aware of budget constraints and key points in schedules. Develop at an early stage adequate procedures for testing designs and equipment. Facilitate early agreement on final designs.

Conflict over personnel resources
Forecast and communicate manpower requirements at an early stage in the planning of the project. Establish detailed manpower requirements with each task group and develop plans for the reallocation of personnel at the end of the project.

Conflict over cost
Forecast costs on a 'best, worst and most likely' basis and discuss effects of each forecast outcome with key administrators. Establish clear objectives for cost control and procedures for monitoring 'sensitive' areas or areas where costs are very uncertain.

Conflict over schedules
Develop a schedule of commitments at an early stage in project planning. With other key administrators, consider the impact of the project on other priority activities of the organization. With task groups, establish work schedules and control performance through regular progress reviews. Look for underutilized project personnel and discuss their reallocation to areas where further help is needed.

Conflict over personalities
Maintain harmonious working relationships by ensuring everyone is

178

aware of their tasks, deadlines and expected performance. Discuss progress regularly. Give careful consideration to the constitution of any task groups where membership is assigned rather than evolved. Ensure that personnel know what their jobs will be at the end of the project, if they are to be retained in the employment of the organization.

Managing conflict

A major role for senior managers and project managers in an organization is the establishment of means for resolving conflict. The procedures outlined above provide a useful framework, but a sensitive approach is still needed. Above all, meetings of senior management to discuss the project should reach agreement on four points: first, the issue to be resolved, secondly, the impact of the issue on the project and the total organization; and thirdly, the alternatives, examined together with the costs and benefits related to each. The final point is that a clear recommendation should be made, and this is vital for the health of the project. It might seem from this list that if the necessary information about cost and benefits of alternative approaches is provided, agreement and a recommendation should quickly follow. Several factors can prevent agreement or bias the agreement in a way which is not supported by the information salient to the issue. First, there may be disagreement about the significance of the data on which the information is based and on its interpretation. The ensuing debate, whilst it may be long and even tedious, is rather helpful because it offers insights into the project objectives and the nature of the expected costs and benefits. It is clearly best if such debate takes place at an early point in the system life cycle, but it is quite likely that fresh insights will be recognized as a project moves through the various phases of the cycle.

A second reason for disagreement on project recommendations may be that one of the disputants is judging the project from the standpoint of personal or technical interest. It is rather difficult to prevent this happening to some extent, because managers are usually well aware of the deficiencies in the services for which they are responsible and can easily spend time trying to solve such problems somewhat out of proportion to the importance of the actual defect. The problem begins to assume a major significance and a potential solution will be seized upon. A judgement, which may not necessarily be shared by others, can thus strongly influence the course of a project. One of the advantages of using a cost—benefit approach is that it provides a common standard for the purposes of comparison, provided there is agreement on the nature

179

of the costs and the value of the benefits. Discussion may be helpful because some mental distance is preserved between the problem, its immediate effects and the proposed solution. On the other hand, the library or information service manager must bear in mind the difficulties associated with imputing value to the project benefits.

The third reason for disagreement arises out of the relationships between members of a group, either as members of a project team, or as senior management. An important aspect of human behaviour is the exercise of power. Some writers suggest that this is what the whole business of life is about. It is certainly true that writing about the management of human behaviour in the settings of social, cultural and work groups and groups in organizations has concentrated on issues such as norms of behaviour, leadership styles and the establishment of power bases as a central factor in the explanation of how such groups operate. It is also true that there are large areas of disagreement over the interpretation of such data as has been collected. There is no unified and coherent theory of human behaviour, and perhaps we are better off without it, but there is an awareness that power seems to be an important component. This is valuable information for the manager because it encourages thought about the behavioural characteristics of the members of the various groups with which contact is maintained. So, one task for a manager is to try to create conditions where power is shared and where personal differences do not obtrude. A counsel of perfection, of course, but some consideration of experience in the software industry may suggest a useful approach.

Programmers often become so interested in the development of the programs for a particular job that they are reluctant to finish and pass them to the customer. Such strong personal identification of a task as 'mine' can have significant advantages because the finished product can benefit from the creative impulse. But two aspects of this identification can put the customer at a disadvantage. First, modifications to the design may be introduced which suit the interests and challenge the expertise and ingenuity of the programmer, but may not, in the end, reflect the needs of the customer. Secondly, such initiative may delay the appearance of the product in a finished and tested form very considerably. To discourage this personal identification but, at the same time, to retain a forum where the benefits of creativity and initiative can be realized, so-called 'egoless' programming teams have been set up, where decision-making, power and responsibility are effectively distributed amongst the members of the team, who meet frequently and work together, sharing problems and discussing the project objectives. Such approaches will only work, however, if there is a set of clear objectives, an agreed timetable and regular project reviews where progress, or the lack of it, has to be demonstrated, explained and justified to senior management or clients.

It may be useful to contrast this approach, sometimes called 'horizontal project management', with the traditional form of project management, the vertical approach. The vertical approach emphasizes a hierarchical chain of command, with power mediated through a series of levels in the project organization. Reports and information flow up and down this structure and it can be a very effective way of dealing with well-defined tasks where the technology or procedures are well understood. Some projects are certainly of this nature: for example, the introduction of a standard computer applications package to solve a well-defined and apparent problem. Where there is uncertainty, where new technology or unusual applications are the focus of developments, then a broader-based, horizontal approach may be best. Such an approach will emphasize the need for sharing of experience and insights and will be fostered best by a team approach, which is largely inimical to hierarchical forms of control. Notice that this does not remove the need for leadership or authority: rather, it encourages each member to assume leadership as that person's specialized skills or knowledge become important to the satisfactory completion of the project. In this way, leadership may be shared, though authority, in the sense of being responsible to a client or senior management, will still be vested in a project manager. It must be acknowledged that team solutions may take more time to develop and may, surprisingly, be slightly less efficient. This is because teams often engage in satisficing behaviour: solutions are selected which suit most of the team members, or least offend their principles, rather than on the basis of which is best. However, a benefit of this approach is that because of greater team commitment it may actually be easier successfully to implement team solutions.

Another way of looking at the problem is to consider the levels of resources needed during the stages of the system life cycle. Consider Figure 25. The message is that the need for each type of resource varies over the system life cycle, but is generally high for all resources during the Design phase when the project team and the organization are experimenting and learning.During this period there is a considerable risk of failure, so this is the point at which a team approach offers considerable advantage. Experience is pooled and insights are shared.

181

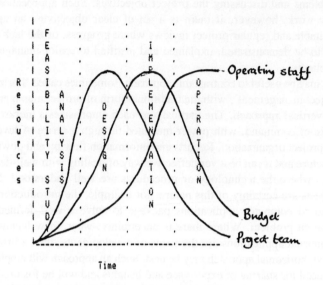

Figure 25   Resource commitment during a project

Uncertainty is faced together. As experience is gained, many of the options are closed off and the direction to be taken becomes more apparent. There is less need for wide-ranging consultation, and more need for firm control to enable deadlines to be met. So, over the life of a single project it may be possible to see the nature and chosen methods of project management changing too.

Is full analysis always necessary?

Another issue in project management is whether it is necessary to analyse every problem or opportunity using the full force of the systems approach. The manager wishing to apply the systems approach has a large selection of tools from which to choose. The question is especially important for project managers, because it cannot be denied that using the full approach will be expensive and time consuming. At the very least, a full project will mean the diversion of considerable resources from other activities and, before committing the organization to this expenditure, senior management must be convinced that it is worthwhile. A useful way of thinking about this is to regard some opportunities or problems as 'time sensitive': that is, success is going to be judged by the speed with which a solution is selected and implemented. Experience and intuition are

182

probably the best guides here. Experience, in particular, connotes the use of means found previously to be successful. The risk of technology failing in such circumstances is fairly low and the costs and benefits are largely known and assured. There is little need for detailed analysis and design but note that, because time has been selected as the critical factor for success, there is an implied constraint on more radical thought and the development of original answers. One may end up with a system that works reliably, but does not quite use the opportunity to full advantage. Such an approach is perfectly defensible: there are many occasions where innovation is neither necessary nor welcome.

Many strategic decisions demand quite another approach: time is not so critical since a middle to long-term view is to be taken. Also, such decisions are often regarded as being 'knowledge sensitive': that is, the environment to which the decision relates is complex and these complex needs require recognition and analysis, followed by sensitive design, implementation and testing. Development time is no longer the criterion for judging success, though it may still be an important factor in selecting a solution.

It is best to regard these two approaches as opposite ends of a continuum. The manager must decide to what extent previous experience can be relied upon as a guide and how important time is to the solution. For each project, a satisfactory mix of horizontal and vertical management styles, team versus individual responsibility and prescriptive rather than consultative management should be decided. A project manager may have a particular favourite style or an organization may have evolved methods of working which have become habitual. It is all too easy to fall in with what has been done before, because it represents a precedent or has previously been judged successful. There may be good reasons for continuing to use such methods, but it should be remembered that the chosen management style may have as much effect on the overall result of the project as the nature of the original problem or opportunity and the efficacy of the technology.

The project team
What about the personal characteristics of the project team and the project manager? The project manager is clearly a key role which requires the ability to balance the elegance and effectiveness of possible technical solutions with time, cost, resource and human factors. In this respect, the project manager is an integrator and a generalist rather than a technical specialist. Such responsibilities represent a tremendous and taxing burden.

Being an integrator implies that one is responsible for the management of a team of specialists, each of which sees a job largely in terms of a personal specialism. The project manager has the job of extracting the common ground from the work of each of the specialists and providing a series of conceptual links which demonstrate how the project meets, or will meet, its overall objectives. Some writers have argued that such approaches are not as successful as might be hoped because it is only the project manager who can see the project as a whole and in its context. As an alternative form of management, the matrix management method has been proposed, whereby functions and responsibilities for technical development and project control are shared amongst the team members, so that each has some responsibility for both.

Perhaps the best advice was written almost two thousand years ago, in a letter from Paul the Apostle to the Christians of Thessalonica: 'We urge you, brothers, warn those who are idle, encourage the timid, help the weak, and be patient with everyone.'

Notes

1   Parkin, A., *Systems management*, London, Edward Arnold, 1980, 70.
2   Adapted from: Thamhain, H. J. and Wilemon, David I., 'Conflict management in project life cycles', *Sloan management review*, **16** (3), 1975, 31−49.

Index

189